ELEMENTARY *Greek*

KOINE FOR BEGINNERS

ELEMENTARY *Greek*

KOINE FOR BEGINNERS

YEAR TWO

With Daily Lesson Plans for a 30 week course

by *Christine Gatchell*

Albuquerque, New Mexico

Published by Open Texture
8200 Montgomery NE No 236
Albuquerque, NM 87109
http://www.opentexture.com

Cover and text design by Susanne Duffner.

Publisher's Cataloging-in-Publication Data

Gatchell, Christine.
    Elementary Greek: Koine for Beginners, Year Two / Christine Gatchell
    p. cm.
    ISBN-10 1-933900-00-8 (pbk)
    ISBN-13 978-1-933900-00-1 (pbk)
    1. Bible. N.T. – Language, style – Problems, exercises, etc.   2. Greek language, Biblical – Grammar Problems, exercises, etc.   3. Greek language, Biblical – Self instruction. I. Title. II. Series.

    PA817.G38   2006   487.4

ISBN-10 1-933900-00-8 (Paperback)
ISBN-13 978-1-933900-00-1 (Paperback)
ISBN-10 1-933900-02-4 (Audio CD)
ISBN-13 978-1-933900-02-5 (Audio CD)
LCCN   2006924278

TABLE OF *contents*

introduction

Welcome back to Elementary Greek. I hope you find Year Two helpful as you and your students continue your Greek studies. The format of this book is very similar to the Year One book, with weekly memory verses, daily lessons, and integrated review. At this level, you will continue to grow in your knowledge of the Greek language as you learn how to use two more noun cases, two verb conjugations, and various prepositions and pronouns. You will find the work slightly more challenging, and so you should be very careful to drill sufficiently. Learning the paradigms thoroughly as they are introduced will keep you from feeling overwhelmed. You may need to spend extra time reviewing these paradigms, which are included in an appendix in the back of the book.

I would encourage you to look into purchasing a Greek or Greek-English interlinear New Testament. This year, two of my boys were feeling weary with their Greek studies. I gave them my standard pep talk about how much they have learned and how well they were doing, and then I pulled out a New Testament for each of them. The pep talk from Mom didn't do a lot to inspire them, but holding those New Testaments did. They immediately began flipping through the pages and calling out words they recognized. We looked up some of our Bible verses. We looked up other verses we have memorized in English to see if we could understand any of the Greek. As you progress in your studies, you will find looking at the actual text very exciting. By the end of this year, you will know about half of the word occurrences in the New Testament. That means that for every two words you read in a given passage, one of them will be familiar to you. You may not recognize the form of the word, and so still be unable to translate it, but you will know that "This word says something about truth" or "That word is a form of ἀκούω."

Also, if you are serious about your Greek study, you may want to get a lexicon. A lexicon is set up like a dictionary, in alphabetical order, with each entry containing the entry word and its definition and range of meaning in English. It goes on to list all New Testament occurrences, as well as some occurrences in other classical Greek writing. A good lexicon will also include pertinent information concerning synonyms and word history. It ties the Koine Greek to the whole history of the Greek language by pointing out similarities between the different dialects, or discussing words which have changed their meaning over time.

I hope that this course continues to help you learn and love the Greek language.

Τῷ δὲ Θεῷ καὶ Πατρὶ ἡμῶν ἡ δόξα εἰς τοὺς αἰῶνας τῶν αἰώνων. ᾿Αμήν.[1]
(Now to our God and Father be glory forever and ever. Amen.)

---

1 All Greek verses in this book are taken from the Majority Text, as found in The NKJV Greek-English Interlinear New Testament. Farstad, Arthur L., et al, eds. Nashville: Thomas Nelson, 1994.

1

The Alphabet

OBJECTIVE:
To review the alphabet and to learn the uncial forms of the letters.

day 1 : The 24 letters of the Greek alphabet

Last year you began by learning the Greek alphabet. To begin this year, we must see how well you remember the Greek letters and the sounds they make. After all, it would be difficult to read anything if you didn't recognize the alphabet in which it was written. All 24 letters of the alphabet in Greek are listed below, along with the letter name and sound(s) they make. By covering the second two columns, you can easily quiz yourself to see how many of the letters you remember.

α	Alpha	/ă/ as in father
β	Beta	/b/
γ	Gamma	/g/ as in get*
δ	Delta	/d/
ε	Epsilon	/ĕ/ as in elephant
ζ	Zeta	/dz/
η	Eta	/ā/ as in ate
θ	Theta	/th/ as in thing
ι	Iota	/ĭ/ as in sit or /ē/ as in be
κ	Kappa	/k/
λ	Lambda	/l/
μ	Mu	/m/
ν	Nu	/n/
ξ	Xi	/x/
ο	Omicron	/ō/ as in obey
π	Pi	/p/
ρ	Rho	/r/
σ,ς	Sigma	/s/*
τ	Tau	/t/
υ	Upsilon	French /ü/ (similar to the English /oo/ sound)
φ	Phi	/f/
χ	Chi	German hard /ch/ as in ach (guttural)

| ψ | | Psi | /ps/ |
| ω | | Omega | /ō/ as in note |

two gammas together say /ng/
The first form of sigma is used in the middle of a word, while the second is used at the end.

Now open your workbook to lesson 1.1 and complete today's practice exercise. Each day, after reading your textbook, you will complete the corresponding assignment in your workbook.

day 2: Uncial Letters

In English, we call uppercase letters capitals. In Greek, they are called uncials. You learned many uncials in your memory work last year, but now we will learn them all to be sure we are familiar with them.

α	A	Alpha	/ă/ as in father
β	B	Beta	/b/
γ	Γ	Gamma	/g/ as in get
δ	Δ	Delta	/d/
ε	E	Epsilon	/ĕ/ as in elephant
ζ	Z	Zeta	/dz/
η	H	Eta	/ā/ as in ate
θ	Θ	Theta	/th/ as in thing
ι	I	Iota	/ĭ/ as in sit or /ē/ as in be
κ	K	Kappa	/k/
λ	Λ	Lambda	/l/
μ	M	Mu	/m/
ν	N	Nu	/n/
ξ	Ξ	Xi	/x/
ο	O	Omicron	/ō/ as in hot
π	Π	Pi	/p/
ρ	P	Rho	/r/
σ,ς	Σ	Sigma	/s/

τ	T	Tau	/t/
υ	Υ	Upsilon	French /ü/ (similar to the English /oo/ sound)
φ	Φ	Phi	/f/
χ	X	Chi	German hard /ch/ as in ach (guttural)
ψ	Ψ	Psi	/ps/
ω	Ω	Omega	/ō/ as in note

As you can see, most of the uncial forms are similar to the lowercase forms. This will make it quite easy for you to learn these. The letters most likely to give you trouble are the gamma, delta, eta, lambda, xi, sigma, upsilon, and omega. Of these, you have seen at least a few of them before. Study this chart until you are able to recognize the uncial forms.

As you will every day, turn to your workbook to complete today's practice exercise.

day 3: Practicing with uncial form

It will still take some time to feel comfortable with the uncial forms. Today in your workbook you will practice by writing the lower case letter for the uncials. Say the letter names and sounds aloud as you come to them.

day 4: Reading words using the uncial form

If you have a Greek New Testament, perhaps you have noticed that the names of the books are written in all capital letters. This can be hard to read if you are not used to it. "KATA MAPKON" is the name for the book of Mark (kata markon, "according to Mark") written just as you will find it in many Greek Bibles. You will read more names of New Testament books in your workbook exercise today.

day 5: Review upper and lower case alphabet

Day 5 is always a review day. Take this day to go over your flashcards, grammar paradigms and memory work. Always check your workbook as well, since most lessons will include a short review exercise.

2

Review of Verbs

OBJECTIVE:
To review the verb paradigms learned in Greek I

day 1: Verb vocabulary

Following are all the regular verbs you learned last year. It is important to make sure you know the material covered last year before beginning to study new vocabulary and grammar. Begin by quizzing yourself on these words. Put any words you don't know on an index card and drill through the week. Quiz yourself on the English and the Greek meanings.

ἀκούω	I hear
βλέπω	I see
ἔχω	I have or hold
λύω	I loose or destroy
πιστεύω	I believe
γινώσκω	I know
γράφω	I write
λαμβάνω	I take
λέγω	I say or speak
πάσχω	I suffer
βάλλω	I throw
διδάσκω	I teach
ἐγείρω	I raise up
ἄγω	I lead
μένω	I remain
πέμπω	I send
φέρω	I bear, bring
βαπτίζω	I baptize
κρίνω	I judge
σώζω	I save
βαίνω	I go
ἁμαρτάνω	I sin
ἀποστέλλω	I send
θέλω	I wish
καλύπτω	I hide

day 2: The conjugation of verbs

Remember that to conjugate a present tense verb, you must know the present tense endings, which indicate person and number. These endings are added onto the verb stem. Last year, you only learned the present tense conjugations, but this year you will be learning two more verb conjugations. The more thoroughly you understand this conjugation, the easier it will be for you to learn the new conjugations.

Present Tense Verb Endings

–ω	*1ˢᵗ person*	–ομεν
–εις	*2ⁿᵈ person*	–ετε
–ει	*3ʳᵈ person*	–ουσι

The endings above can be translated into English subject pronouns:

I	*1ˢᵗ person*	we
you	*2ⁿᵈ person*	you (plural)
he, she, it	*3ʳᵈ person*	they

Using these endings, orally conjugate the first five words on the vocabulary list above. Be sure you also know the English meanings for these conjugations.

day 3: The irregular verb εἰμί

Not all verbs follow the regular conjugation above. In English, we have many, many irregular verbs. But Greek is much simpler than English in this regard, because there are very few irregular verbs in Greek. Right now, we are concerned with only one of these verbs, the word εἰμί. This word, which means "I am," does not use the same conjugation endings written above.

Read through the conjugation for εἰμί:

εἰμί	*1ˢᵗ person*	ἐσμέν
εἶ	*2ⁿᵈ person*	ἐστέ
ἐστί	*3ʳᵈ person*	εἰσί

Orally conjugate βάλλω, διδάσκω, and ἐγείρω.

day 4: Using verbs

Whenever a verb is encountered, it must be thought of as a pronoun-verb combination. Remember that each of the present tense verb endings you have reviewed this week has a meaning. Each of them stands for a specific subject pronoun. When we translate the following verbs, we must include the subject pronouns.

βάλλομεν

We can see that the first person plural ending –ομεν has been added to the stem βαλλ–, meaning "throw". This tells us to read the verb as, "we throw".

λύεις

Again, find the meaning of the ending –εις and of the stem λυ–. We can then translate the verb as, "you loose".

The ease with which you do this will show how well you know and understand the present tense verb conjugation. If today's exercise is difficult for you to do, be sure to take the time to study and learn the charts above before you proceed to the next lesson.

day 5: Review vocabulary

You should know the English translations for all of these words without looking at the list above.

ἀκούω   βλέπω
ἔχω   λύω
πιστεύω   γινώσκω
γράφω   λαμβάνω
λέγω   πάσχω

βάλλω   διδάσκω
ἐγείρω   ἄγω
μένω   πέμπω
φέρω   βαπτίζω
κρίνω   σώζω

βαίνω
ἁμαρτάνω
ἀποστέλλω
θέλω
καλύπτω

3

Review of Second Declension Nouns

OBJECTIVE:
to review the paradigms which are part of the second declension

day 1 : Second declension masculine noun vocabulary

Following are all the second declension masculine nouns you learned last year. It is important to make sure you know the material covered last year before beginning to study new vocabulary and grammar. Begin by quizzing yourself on these words. Any words you don't know, put on an index card and drill through the week. Quiz yourself on the English and the Greek meanings.

ὁ ἄγγελος	the messenger, angel
ὁ λόγος	the word
ὁ νόμος	the law
ὁ βίος	the life
ὁ θεός	the God
ὁ ἀγρός	the field
ὁ ἀπόστολος	the apostle
ὁ ἀδελφός	the brother
ὁ ἄνθρωπος	the man
ὁ δοῦλος	the slave
ὁ κόσμος	the world
ὁ θάνατος	the death
ὁ οἶκος	the house
ὁ υἱός	the son
ὁ κύριος	the lord
ὁ λίθος	the stone
ὁ οὐρανός	the heaven
ὁ τόπος	the place
ὁ διδάσκαλος	the teacher
ὁ ἁμαρτωλός	the sinner
ὁ ἄρτος	the bread
ὁ τυφλός	the blind man
ὁ Ἰουδαῖος	the Jew

ὁ καρπός	the fruit
ὁ Φαρισαῖος	the Pharisee
ὁ Χριστός	the Christ

day 2: Second declension masculine paradigm

Just as verbs have conjugations, nouns have declensions. There are three declensions in Greek, and we learn the simplest one first. The second declension masculine endings follow:

singular		*plural*
–ος	Nominative	–οι
–ου	Genitive	–ων
–ῳ	Dative	–οις
–ον	Accusative	–ους

Added to a stem word, they look like this:

singular		*plural*
ἄνθρωπος	Nominative	ἄνθρωποι
ἀνθρώπου	Genitive	ἀνθρώπων
ἀνθρώπῳ	Dative	ἀνθρώποις
ἄνθρωπον	Accusative	ἀνθρώπους

Last year you learned that the nominative case is used for the subject or predicate nominative in a sentence. Using the chart above as a sample, the translation would be *man/men*. You also learned that the genitive case is used to show possession. Remember that the genitive is translated as *of a man/of men*.

day 3: Second declension neuter vocabulary

These words are also part of the second declension. Review them to be sure that you remember them from your studies last year. Continue to quiz yourself on any you miss.

τό τέκνον	the child
τό εὐαγγέλιον	the gospel
τό πρόσωπον	the face
τό ἱερόν	the temple
τό δῶρον	the gift
τό βιβλίον	the book
τό δαιμόνιον	the demon
τό ἔργον	the work
τό πλοῖον	the boat

day 4: Second declension neuter paradigm

Nouns in Greek have gender. This means that they are either masculine, feminine, or neuter. Some nouns have obvious genders: the word ἄνθρωπος (*man*) is a masculine noun and the word γυνή (*woman*) is feminine. However, the gender of most words seems arbitrary, especially to English-speaking people, since we do not have this concept in our language. This means that the gender for many words must simply be memorized.

You have learned the paradigm for second-declension masculine nouns, and now you will review the paradigm for second-declension neuter nouns. These are the only two sets of endings in the second declension, which is why it is considered the easiest to learn. There are a few feminine nouns which are part of the second declension, but they use the same endings that the masculine nouns use.[1]

---

1 Perhaps you recall learning two of these words last year. They are ἡ ἔρημος (the desert) and ἡ ὁδός (the road, the way).

The second-declension neuter endings:

singular		plural
–ον	Nominative	–α
–ου	Genitive	–ων
–ῳ	Dative	–οις
–ον	Accusative	–α

There are a few things which make these endings very easy to remember. First, notice that the nominative and the accusative endings are identical, both on the singular and the plural side. That leaves only the genitive and dative endings to learn, but once you look at them, you will realize that they are the same genitive and dative endings you have already learned in the masculine paradigm. Here is what the endings look like once they are added onto a stem:

singular		plural
δῶρον	Nominative	δῶρα
δώρου	Genitive	δώρων
δώρῳ	Dative	δώροις
δῶρον	Accusative	δῶρα

day 5: Review vocabulary

You should know the English translations for all of these words without looking at the lists above.

ὁ ἄγγελος	ὁ λόγος
ὁ νόμος	ὁ βίος
ὁ θεός	ὁ ἀγρός
ὁ ἀπόστολος	ὁ ἀδελφός
ὁ ἄνθρωπος	ὁ δοῦλος

ὁ κόσμος	ὁ θάνατος
ὁ οἶκος	ὁ υἱός
ὁ κύριος	ὁ λίθος
ὁ οὐρανός	ὁ τόπος

4

Review of First Declension Nouns

OBJECTIVE:
to review the paradigms which are part of the first declension

day 1: First declension feminine noun vocabulary

The following list contains all of the first declension nouns we covered last year. Review these and be sure you know them both in English and Greek.

ἡ ἀλήθεια	the truth
ἡ βασιλεία	the kingdom
ἡ ἐκκλησία	the church
ἡ ἡμέρα	the day
ἡ ὥρα	the hour
ἡ καρδία	the heart
ἡ γραφή	the writing/scripture
ἡ παραβολή	the parable
ἡ εἰρήνη	the peace
ἡ ἐντολή	the commandment
ἡ ζωή	the life
ἡ φωνή	the voice
ἡ ψυχή	the soul/life
ἡ ἀγάπη	the love
ἡ ἁμαρτία	the sin
ἡ ἐπαγγελία	the promise
ἡ χαρά	the joy
ἡ οἰκία	the house

day 2: First declension paradigms

While the second declension has only two variations of endings, there are five variations in the first declension. This may seem overwhelming at first, but really the differences between the sets of endings are minor and easily mastered. At this point, we have only learned two of these variations, so these are the only two we will be reviewing today. The chart of endings below shows how a first declension noun ending in *alpha* is declined. But you will recall that several of the vocabulary words you have learned actually end in *eta*. To know how to decline these nouns, remember this rule:

First declension nouns ending in eta keep the eta in all the singular endings.

The plural endings are identical, whether the singular nominative form ends in alpha or eta.

singular		plural
–α	Nominative	–αι
–ας	Genitive	–ων
–ᾳ	Dative	–αις
–αν	Accusative	–ας

Here are two key words, declined in all four cases.

singular		plural
ἀλήθεια	Nominative	ἀλήθειαι
ἀληθείας	Genitive	ἀλήθειῶν
ἀληθείᾳ	Dative	ἀληθείαις
ἀλήθειαν	Accusative	ἀληθείας
γραφή	Nominative	γραφαί
γραφῆς	Genitive	γραφῶν
γραφῇ	Dative	γραφαῖς
γραφήν	Accusative	γραφάς

day 3 : Parsing gender, number, and case

The following words are declined, just as you will see them in various sentences you will be required to translate. The more comfortable you are in determining the gender, number, and case of a given word, the more easily you will be able to translate sentences.

καρδιῶν

Find the gender (masculine, feminine, neuter).
καρδία is a feminine word.

Find the number (singular, plural) and case (nominative, genitive, dative, accusative). The ending –ων is plural and genitive.

We can now translate καρδιῶν as "hearts".

The cases help to identify the primary 'job' of a noun in the sentence, so that καρδιῶν, with its genitive ending, would be used to show possession, "of hearts". For now, since you have not learned the typical translations for all the cases, you can simply give a straight translation of the word, taking into account the distinction between singular and plural.

Now look at:
δώροις

We need to identify its gender, number, and case and provide a translation. We remember that it is a neuter noun, plural, and dative. Since we have not yet learned the primary uses of the dative case, we will translate it simply as "gifts".

	gender	number	case	translation
καρδιῶν	F	P	Gen.	hearts
δώροις	N	P	Dat.	gifts

day 4: Translating Sentences

Last year you spent a lot of time translating sentences, using the nominative and genitive cases of nouns. This year you will continue translating, and you will also begin using the dative and accusative cases. For today, you have several sentences to translate into English. These sentences will use the nominative and genitive cases as you learned them last year. Remember to find the nouns and then look at their endings to identify their jobs in these sentences.

day 5: Review vocabulary

You should be able to translate every word on this list:

ἡ ἀλήθεια	ἡ βασιλεία
ἡ ἐκκλησία	ἡ ἡμέρα
ἡ ὥρα	ἡ δόξα
ἡ καρδία	ἡ γραφή
ἡ παραβολή	ἡ εἰρήνη
ἡ ἐντολή	ἡ ζωή
ἡ φωνή	ἡ ψυχή
ἡ ἀγάπη	ἡ ἁμαρτία
ἡ ἐπαγγελία	ἡ χαρά
ἡ οἰκία	

5

Review of Adjectives and Prepositions

OBJECTIVE: to review the rules for declining and using adjectives, and the use of prepositions

day 1 : Vocabulary

These are the adjectives and prepositions you learned last year. Be sure you know how to translate them from Greek to English and from English to Greek. Any that you do not know, review over the course of the week.

ἀγαθός	good (moral)
ἄλλος	other
ἔσχατος	last
κακός	bad
καλός	good, beautiful
πιστός	faithful
πρῶτος	first
δίκαιος	righteous
δεύτερος	second
ἅγιος	holy

ἀπό	(with the genitive)	from
διά	(with the genitive)	through
ἐκ/ἐξ	(with the genitive)	out of
μετά	(with the genitive)	with
κατά	(with the genitive)	against
παρά	(with the genitive)	from
περί	(with the genitive)	about
πρό	(with the genitive)	before

day 2 : Formation of adjectives

An adjective is a descriptive word. It modifies a noun by telling us something more about the noun. Words for numbers, colors, and qualities are all adjectives.

In Greek, most adjectives must *agree* with the noun they modify.[1] *Agree* means that the adjective must have the same gender, number, and case as the noun. If a noun is masculine, singular, and in the accusative case, then the adjective modifying it must also be masculine, singular, and in the accusative case. This means that all adjectives can be masculine, feminine, or neuter. You can see this on the chart below. This chart should be read by columns. First read the masculine singular column, then the feminine, and then the neuter. Then proceed to the plural side. Last year you only memorized the nominative and genitive endings for adjectives. Within the next few weeks, you will be continuing to learn the dative and accusative endings as well. This is a chart of the declension for ἀγαθός, *good*.

	Singular				*Plural*		
masc.	*fem.*	*neut.*		*masc.*	*fem.*	*neut.*
ἀγαθός	ἀγαθη	ἀγαθόν	N	ἀγαθοί	ἀγαθαί	ἀγαθά
ἀγαθοῦ	ἀγαθῆς	ἀγαθοῦ	G	ἀγαθῶν	ἀγαθῶν	ἀγαθῶν
ἀγαθῷ	ἀγαθη	ἀγαθω	D	ἀγαθοῖς	ἀγαθαῖς	ἀγαθοῖς
ἀγαθόν	ἀγαθήν	ἀγαθόν	G	ἀγαθούς	ἀγαθάς	ἀγαθά

Remember that the feminine singular endings will use an eta *unless* the stem ends in an ι, ε, or ρ, in which case the endings will use an alpha.

day 3: Using adjectives

An adjective can be placed in Greek either before or after a noun. Remember that in Greek, sentence structure is a lot more fluid than it is in English. So, while it is unusual in English to say, "a man faithful," it is quite common to find "ἄνθρωπος πιστός" in Greek sentences. The endings on the adjectives make it clear which noun they are modifying in a sentence, even if they are not found directly before the noun.[1]

---

1 There is an important grammatical point, which is beyond the scope of this course, but interesting nonetheless. The adjective can be either in an attributive position (The good man) or in a predicate position (The man is good). This difference, in the Greek language, is often indicated by the use of the article. If the article comes right before the adjective, the adjective is attributive. ὁ ἀγαθὸς ἄνθρωπος and ὁ ἄνθρωπος ὁ ἀγαθός are two examples of this. Notice how the article is repeated in the second example so that it comes immediately before the adjective. If the article does not immediately precede the adjective, then the adjective is in the predicate position, even when the linking verb is omitted. So, ἀγαθὸς ὁ ἄνθρωπος and ὁ ἄνθρωπος ἀγαθὸς both mean "The man is good." Because there is no indefinite article in Greek, this distinction cannot be seen in a phrase such as "A good man" or "A man is good." Other information must be used to determine which is meant by ἀγαθὸς ἄνθρωπος or ἄνθρωπος ἀγαθός. In this lesson, all the adjectives are meant to be attributive.

Today you will modify nouns by adding a correctly declined adjective. Remember that for the feminine nouns you have learned, the adjective ending will not always have the same vowel (alpha or eta) as the noun. *Remember the rule you have learned to determine which vowel to use in the singular feminine endings.*

day 4: Using prepositions with the genitive

Last year you began to learn about prepositions. Can you give a definition of a preposition? Can you give an example?

A preposition is a word that shows the relationship between a noun and the rest of the sentence. *About, above, around* are all prepositions.

Remember that whenever you use the prepositions you reviewed at the beginning of this lesson, the **object of the preposition** (the noun that follows the preposition) must be in the genitive case. In the next few weeks, we will be learning some new prepositions, which will need their objects to take nouns in the dative and accusative cases.

The man went out of the store.

In the sentence above, the phrase *out of* is easily identified as the preposition. If you ask, "Out of what?" you find that the answer to your question (store) is the object of the preposition. In Greek, this word would be in the genitive case.

day 5: Review vocabulary

The following story includes many of your vocabulary words. Can you read the story and answer the questions?

ὁ ἀγαθὸς υἱὸς βαίνει διὰ τοῦ ἀγροῦ. βαίνει μετὰ τοῦ ἀποστόλου. ὁ ἀπόστολός ἐστι διδάσκαλος ἀληθείας. διδάσκει περὶ θεοῦ. ὁ υἱὸς καὶ ὁ ἀπόστολός εἰσι πιστοὶ ἄνθρωποι.

Where does the good son go?

Who does he go with?

What does the apostle teach the son?

Who are faithful men?

Next week, you will be beginning new material. Be sure you feel comfortable with the review lessons before you go forward.

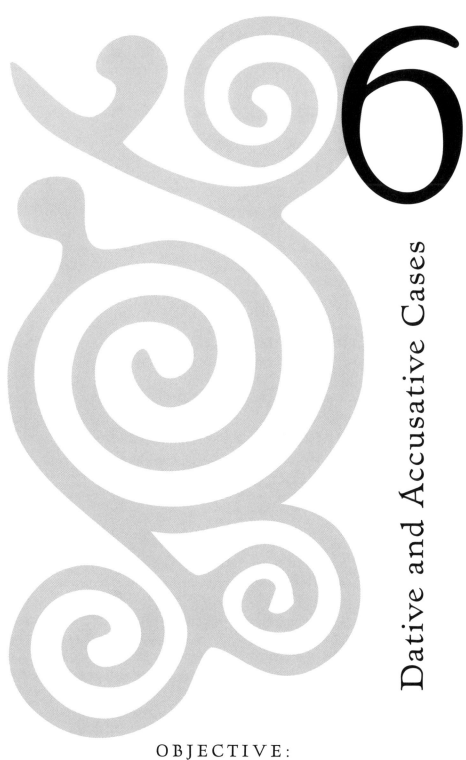

6

Dative and Accusative Cases

OBJECTIVE:
To become familiar with the dative and accusative case

Memory Verse:

Ἡ ἀγάπη οὐδέποτε ἐκπίπτει.

Love   never   fails.

I Corinthians 13:8

Our first memory verse for this year comes from the book of I Corinthians (ΠΡΟΣ ΚΟΡΙΝΘΙΟΥΣ Α). The verse is short, but do not rush through in your reading of it. You want to be sure to pronounce each word carefully and clearly. This will help you to memorize and remember the verse.[1]

day 1 : Introduction to dative and accusative cases.

When you learned the paradigms for first and second declension nouns last year, you learned four cases. Your second declension masculine paradigm looks like this:

ἄνθρωπος	N	ἄνθρωποι
ἀνθρώπου	G	ἀνθρώπων
ἀνθρώπῳ	D	ἀνθρώποις
ἄνθρωπον	A	ἀνθρώπους

You learned that the first line is called the nominative case, and it shows us the subject or predicate nominative of the sentence. The second line is called the genitive. It shows us the possessive in a sentence, and it is also used as the object of a preposition. Now look carefully at the third line down. This is the line for the dative case. The dative case singular has –ῳ for an ending, and the plural has –οις. Then look at the final line, which is the accusative case. Notice the endings are –ον and –ους. Now read through the entire declension, from start to finish. Both the dative and the accusative cases have their own jobs in the sentence.

---

1 Although the word *the* (Ἡ) is used in the original Greek, it is left out in the English translation. It is common in Greek for abstract nouns to include the article, although it is not common in English.

Recite the endings for the second declension neuter. Notice that the dative and the accusative endings are the same as the masculine, except in the accusative plural. The neuter accusative plural ends in alpha.

day 2: Recognizing the dative and accusative

Today you will *parse* nouns by indicating their case, number, and gender before translating. Refer to your charts if necessary as you grow accustomed to identifying datives and accusatives.

day 3: Recognizing dative and accusative in the first declension.

Of course, first declension nouns use the dative and accusative case too. Here is the paradigm for the first declension:

singular		*plural*
ἀλήθεια	N	ἀλήθειαι
ἀληθείας	G	ἀληθειῶν
ἀληθείᾳ	D	ἀληθείαις
ἀλήθειαν	A	ἀληθείας

Remember that in the first declension, there are two possible endings on the singular side, but the plural side has only one set of endings.

What are the first declension dative singular endings?

What is the dative plural ending?

What are the accusative singular endings?

What is the accusative plural ending?

day 4: Recognizing all four cases

The easier it is for you to quickly parse a noun (to recognize its gender, number, and case), the more you will enjoy translation exercises. With that in mind, today's workbook assignment requires you to use all the information you have acquired so far to determine gender (masculine, feminine, neuter), number (singular, plural), and case (nominative, genitive, dative, accusative) of these words. All genders and cases are included in this exercise. In the instance of two cases sharing the same ending, list both cases under the appropriate column. You may need to refer to your charts to complete the exercise, but remember that you are to be working toward mastery in the memorization of these charts.

day 5: Review paradigms for nouns, adjectives, and present tense verbs.

7

The Direct Object

O B J E C T I V E : To learn the case used for direct object

Memory Verse:

Ἡ ἀγάπη οὐδέποτε ἐκπίπτει.

Love   never   fails.

I Corinthians 13:8

day 1 : Vocabulary.

In each lesson, you will be introduced to five new vocabulary words. In addition, you will have five words from last year to review. This will help you to add to your vocabulary base without forgetting those words you have already learned. Study these words carefully, and remember to review them throughout the week.

ἡ ἀρχή	the beginning
ἐκβάλλω	I cast out
ἡ χώρα	the country
ὁ ὄχλος	the crowd
πίπτω	I fall

Notice that the word πίπτω, one of your vocabulary words this week, is a part of your memory verse as well. You will notice that in your memory verse it has a prefix attached to it. This prefix you may recognize as one of the prepositions you reviewed just a few weeks ago—ἐκ (out of). Of course, to be used correctly in the sentence, the verb must also be conjugated, in this case with the third person singular ending (ει) to agree with the subject of the sentence, *love*. ἐκπίπτω is very similar to one of your other vocabulary words this week as well. ἐκβάλλω combines the verb βάλλω, which you are already familiar with, with the prefix ἐκ to give you a new word meaning *I cast (or throw) out.*

Review vocabulary:

ὁ ἄγγελος	the messenger, angel
ὁ λόγος	the word
βάλλω	I throw

| διδάσκω | I teach |
| δέκα | ten |

Quiz yourself on these words.

day 2: Recognizing direct objects

In English, you have probably learned about **direct objects.** Can you define what a direct object is? How do we find a direct object in a sentence?

A direct object usually comes after the verb. This is true in English and in Greek. Although Greek is inflected and therefore has more flexibility regarding sentence structure, most sentences do follow the S-V-DO pattern that we are used to seeing in English sentences. The direct object answers the question *who or what?* about the verb. In these sentences, find the nouns that are used as a direct object. Remember that a **direct object** must be a **noun.**

Jesus cast out demons.

Find the verb: *cast out.* Ask the question, "He cast out *what?*" The answer, demons, is your direct object.

My aunt sees elephants at the zoo.

She sees what? Elephants.

Somehow, I will win the race.

Judy ate pancakes.

The Greeks conquered Macedonia.

day 3: Formation of the direct object in Greek

In Greek, we use a special case to show that a noun is being used as a direct object in a sentence. You already know that we must use the nominative case to show that a noun is the subject of a sentence. You also know that the genitive case shows possession. But if we want a noun to be the **direct object** in the sentence,

we must use the **accusative case** for that noun.

day 4: Translating sentences

Today we will try translating some simple sentences with direct objects. Classify the sentences by marking the subject (S), verb (V), and direct object (DO) first. Remember to use the proper case endings as you translate.

day 5: Review vocabulary

8

The Direct Object

OBJECTIVE : To continue using the direct object and to become familiar with its characteristics in Greek.

Memory Verse:

Ὁ λόγος ὁ σὸς ἀλήθειά[1] ἐστι.

The word Your truth is.

ΚΑΤΑ ΙΩΑΝΝΗΝ 17:17
(According to) John 17:17

In your English Bible, you will find that this verse is translated, *Your word is truth*. As you work on memorizing this, pay attention to the fact that ὁ λόγος ὁ σὸς is a phrase. These words all go together to give us the English *your word*. Notice that the endings on λόγος and σὸς are the same, making it clear that σὸς is modifying λόγος. It would be incorrect to translate this verse, *The word is your truth*. The masculine nominative ending on σὸς shows that it cannot modify the feminine nominative ἀλήθειά.

day 1 : Vocabulary

Review past Bible verses.

ἡ ἀδελφή	the sister
ἡ θύρα	the door
ἡ πέτρα	the rock
ὁ σταυρός	the cross
ἡ τιμή	the honor

Perhaps you have read Matthew 16:18 before. This is the verse that records Jesus giving Simon the special name of Peter. "And I also say to you that you are Peter, and on this rock I will build my church...." The name Peter comes from the Greek word for rock, πέτρα.

---

1 You may have noticed that the word ἀλήθειά has two accents, although most Greek words have only one. There are certain words (called **enclitics**) that sometimes cause other words to have two accents. An enclitic is a word that has no accent of its own. Instead, its accent is absorbed by the word preceding it. In this case, the word ἐστι is enclitic—its accent has been shifted back so that it sits on the final syllable of ἀλήθειά. Sometimes the preceding word carries its own accent and the accent of the enclitic, and sometimes the accent from the enclitic and the accent on the preceding word are combined to form one accent.

Review vocabulary:

ὁ νόμος	the law
ὁ βίος	the life
ὁ θεός	the God
ὁ ἀγρός	the field
ὁ ἀπόστολος	the apostle

day 2: Parsing nouns

So far you have learned the primary uses of three of the four noun cases. You should be able to recall two uses for the nominative case, and one each for the genitive and accusative cases. Could you explain those uses to someone else?

day 3: Translating sentences from English to Greek

Today you will classify sentences and translate them into Greek. You will need to use the nominative, genitive, and accusative cases as appropriate for the role each noun plays in the sentence.

Which case will you use for the subject?
Which case will you use for the direct object?
For possessives?

day 4: Translating sentences from English to Greek

Today as you translate sentences from Greek to English, remember that the case endings will tell you what each noun's job is in the sentence.

day 5: Review vocabulary

9

Prepositions with the Dative and Accusative

OBJECTIVE: To learn several prepositions which require either the dative or the accusative case as their objects

Memory Verse:

Ὁ λόγος ὁ σὸς ἀλήθειά ἐστι.

The   word   Your   truth   is.

ΚΑΤΑ ΙΩΑΝΝΗΝ 17:17
(According to) John 17:17

day 1: Vocabulary

Review past Bible verses.

ἐν	(with the dative)	in
σύν	(with the dative)	with
εἰς	(with the accusative)	into
ὑπό	(with the accusative)	under
ὑπέρ	(with the accusative)	above

Read through these words several times, and then quiz yourself on them. Remember to say which case you need to use with the preposition whenever you say the preposition. **Never** say 'ἐν', but **always** say 'ἐν with the dative.' Every day quiz yourself on these words, as well as any words you still don't know from the past few weeks.

Review vocabulary:

ὁ ἀδελφός	the brother
ὁ ἄνθρωπος	the man
ὁ δοῦλος	the slave
ὁ κόσμος	the world
καί	and

day 2: Parsing nouns

You have begun learning about the dative and accusative cases. Today, we are going to review what you have learned by continuing to parse nouns. Remember to begin by thinking of the words in their **nominative** form (This is the form you have memorized in your vocabulary lists)[1]. This will tell you whether the word is masculine, feminine, or neuter. The masculine nouns which you have learned so far end in –ος, the neuter nouns end in –ον, and the feminine nouns end in –α.

day 3: Recognizing and translating prepositional phrases

Last year, you learned how to write prepositional phrases in Greek. A prepositional phrase must have a preposition and an object of the preposition. Here are some examples of prepositional phrases in English.

into a temple

in churches

with God

under a stone

above angels

In each of the above phrases, find the preposition and the object of the preposition.

In Greek, the object of the preposition must be in a certain case. The case changes depending on which preposition we are using. Every preposition you used last year took the genitive case, but if you go back and look at this week's vocabulary words, you will see that prepositions can also take the dative and the accusative cases. This is why you must always memorize prepositions together with the case they take.

---

1 The 'vocabulary form' that we refer to is also called the lexical form. This is the form of the word that is used as the entry word in lexicons and dictionaries.

day 4: Translating from English to Greek

Today you will translate sentences from English to Greek. Remember to classify your sentence first by marking the parts of speech. Above each word, indicate whether it is a:

subject (S)
verb (V)
direct object (DO)
preposition (prep)
object of the preposition (OP)

day 5: Review vocabulary

10

Review

OBJECTIVE:
To review concepts taught in the last five lessons

day 1: Vocabulary and Bible verse review

Begin by reciting I Corinthians 13:8 and John 17:17. You should have both of these verses completely memorized.

Vocabulary:

ἡ ἀρχή	the beginning
ἐκβάλλω	I cast out
ἡ χώρα	the country
ὁ ὄχλος	the crowd
πίπτω	I fall
ἡ ἀδελφή	the sister
ἡ θύρα	the door
ἡ πέτρα	the rock
ὁ σταυρός	the cross
ἡ τιμή	the honor
ἐν (with the dative)	in
σύν (with the dative)	with
εἰς (with the accusative)	into
ὑπό (with the accusative)	under
ὑπέρ (with the accusative)	above

Quiz yourself on the words above. Spend extra time studying any that you didn't remember.

day 2: Translating prepositional phrases

Today you will translate prepositional phrases from Greek to English. Note the case endings for the object of each preposition.

day 3: Translating from Greek to English

Yesterday you practiced translating prepositional phrases from Greek to English. Today you will see phrases like those as part of complete sentences. Classifying the parts of speech before you translate will help you to see how those parts work together. Above each word, indicate whether it is a:

subject (S)
verb (V)
direct object (DO)
adjective (adj)
preposition (prep)
object of the preposition (OP)

day 4: Translating from Greek to English

Continue to translate sentences from Greek to English.

day 5: Review vocabulary

See if you can read and understand this short paragraph. Answer the questions below.

> ἐν τῇ ἀρχῇ, ὁ ἄνθρωπος διδάσκει τὸν δοῦλον περὶ τοῦ ἀγροῦ καὶ περὶ τῶν πέτρων. οἱ πέτροι εἰσὶν ἐν τῷ ἀγρῷ. ὁ δοῦλος βάλλει δέκα πέτρας ἐκ τοῦ ἀγροῦ. ὁ ἄνθρωπος κρίνει τὸ καλὸν ἔργον τοῦ δούλου. ὁ δοῦλος ἔχει τὴν τιμήν.

What does the man teach the slave?

How many rocks does the slave throw out of the field?

Does the man like the slave's work? How do you know?

11

Article 'the'

OBJECTIVE:
To learn the entire paradigm for the article adjective 'the'

Memory Verse:

Δόξα ἐν ὑψίστοις Θεῷ,

Glory in (the) heights to God,

ΚΑΤΑ ΛΟΥΚΑΝ 2:14a
(According to)Luke 2:14a

This is your first week learning Luke 2:14, which is composed of three phrases. On the day Christ was born, the angels appeared to the shepherds on the hills, singing, "Glory to God in the highest, and on earth peace, goodwill toward men!" This week, you will learn to say "Glory to God in the highest" as it is written in the Greek New Testament.

day 1 : Vocabulary

Review past Bible verses.

ἄρχω	I rule
ἀναβαίνω	I go up
καταβαίνω	I go down
αἴρω	I take up, I take away
ἐσθίω	I eat

Notice that two of your words are similar to another vocabulary word you have already learned. Can you find the words I am talking about? Last year, you learned that βαίνω means 'I go'. Looking at this week's vocabulary words, you can see that by adding prefixes onto the word βαίνω, you can change the meaning of the word. ἀναβαίνω means 'I go up' (ανα- means *up*), and καταβαίνω means 'I go down.' (You have learned that κατα means *against*, but now you can see that it can also mean *down*.)

Review vocabulary:

ἡ ἔρημος		the desert
ἡ ὁδός		the road, the way
κατά	(with the genitive)	against
παρά	(with the genitive)	from
περί	(with the genitive)	about

These words are all from the vocabulary lists in Greek I. It is important that you continue to review them.

day 2: The complete paradigm for the article

Last year, you learned how to say the word 'the' in the nominative and genitive cases. This week, we are going to finish learning this chart. That means that we must learn the word 'the' in the dative and accusative cases. Here is the entire chart. Read it through several times, first down each column on the left side, and then down the right-side columns.

masc.	*fem.*	*neut.*		*masc.*	*fem.*	*neut.*
ὁ	ἡ	το	N	οἱ	αι	τά
τοῦ	τῆς	τοῦ	G	τῶν	τῶν	τῶν
τῶ	τῇ	τῷ	D	τοῖς	ταῖς	τοῖς
τόν	τήν	τό	A	τούς	τάς	τά

Notice the similarities between the article and the regular noun endings. In most cases they are exactly the same. That will make it very easy to memorize this table!

day 3: Using the forms of the article

Remember that whenever we use the word 'the', we must be sure that it agrees with the noun in gender, number, and case.

day 4 : Translate sentences from Greek to English

Today you will translate some sentences from Greek into English. When you classify, mark the article as 'art'.

day 5 : Review vocabulary

12

The Word 'Not'

Memory Verse:

Δόξα ἐν ὑψίστοις Θεῷ,

Glory   in   (the) heights   to God,

Καὶ ἐπὶ γῆς εἰρήνη,

And   on   earth   peace,

KATA ΛOYKAN 2:14a,b
(According to)Luke 2:14a,b

day 1 : Vocabulary.

Review past Bible verses.

κηρύσσω	I preach
πείθω	I persuade
ἡ φυλακή	the prison
ἡ δικαιοσύνη	the righteousness
οὐ	not

Can you identify the part of speech of each of the words above?

Review vocabulary:

ἀπό	(with the genitive)	from
διά	(with the genitive)	through
ἐκ/ἐξ	(with the genitive)	out of
μετά	(with the genitive)	with
κατά	(with the genitive)	against

day 2: Negating words in Greek

This week you have a new kind of word in your vocabulary. Can you find it? It is the word *not,* οὐ. You may have learned in your English classes that *not* **is not a verb.** Remember that *not* is actually an adverb. In Greek, *not* is a very simple, short word. But just like we sometimes change our word *a* to *an,* the Greeks would change their word οὐ (for *not*) to οὐκ. Sometimes they would even change it to οὐχ. Why do we change *a* to *an*? Because sometimes just *a* is hard to say. Try to say "A owl." Now say "An owl." See how much easier it is to say "An owl?" Now try to say, "οὐ ἀκούω." As you can see, this also is hard to say. So the Greeks added a kappa to the end of this word to make it easier to say when it came before a vowel. Say "οὐκ ἀκούω." When the vowel on the word after the word *not* had a rough breathing mark, like the word ἁμαρτάνω, the Greek has a chi at the end of the word *not:* οὐχ. See how that makes οὐχ ἁμαρτάνω easier to say?

Today you will negate some Greek verbs, and then translate. To negate the words, insert the Greek word for *not* in the space before the word. Remember that you must decide between the three forms of the word: οὐ, οὐκ, οὐχ.

day 3: Translate sentences from English to Greek

To use *not* in a sentence, you put it before the word you want to negate. This is the same thing you do in English. I do not say, "I run not," but rather "I do not run." *Not* is describing run, so it goes before the word run. Remember that *not is not a verb,* and mark it 'adv' for adverb when you are classifying your sentences.

day 4: Translate from Greek to English

Translate sentences including forms of the word 'οὐ' from Greek into English. Above each word, indicate whether it is a:

subject (S)
verb (V)

direct object (DO)
adjective (adj)
preposition (prep)
object of the preposition (OP)
article (art)
adverb (adv)

Remember to classify forms of the word 'ου' as adverbs.

day 5: Review vocabulary

13

Personal Pronouns

OBJECTIVE:
To begin memorizing paradigms for personal pronouns

Memory Verse:

Δόξα ἐν ὑψίστοις Θεῷ,
Glory   in   (the) heights   to God,

Καὶ ἐπὶ γῆς εἰρήνη,
And   on   earth   peace,

Ἐν ἀνθρώποις εὐδοκία!
Among   men   good will!

ΚΑΤΑ ΛΟΥΚΑΝ 2:14
(According to)Luke 2:14

day 1: Vocabulary.

Review past Bible verses.

ἐγώ	I
σύ	you
ἀμήν	verily, truly, amen
μόνος	alone, only
ὁ χρόνος	the time

Two of your vocabulary words are pronouns. Usually, the pronoun which is used as the subject of the sentence is included in the verb as an ending. Think of ἀποστέλλομεν or πιστεύετε. But sometimes, if we really want to emphasize the pronoun, we can also use a separate word for the pronoun. Think of your memory verse, John 14:6. How does it begin? ἐγώ εἰμι ἡ ὁδος (I, I am the way). This week, we will begin memorizing the paradigm for the pronoun *I*. Pronouns, like nouns, are declined.

You also have three more words in your vocabulary list. As you can see, our word *amen* comes directly from the Greek ἀμήν. The word is transliterated from the

Greek, which means that the Greek letters have been changed to English letters, but the word itself has stayed the same.

Have you ever heard of the English word *chronology*? It refers to the arranging of things or events in the order in which they occurred. Which of the words above do you think it comes from? What about the English word *monologue*, which means a speech by one person?

Review vocabulary:

δίκαιος	righteous
νεκρός	dead
δεύτερος	second
ὁ Φαρισαῖος	the Pharisee
ἀποστέλλω	I send

day 2: Paradigm for personal pronoun *I*

This week we will begin learning a new paradigm. *Paradigm* is just a technical name for memory chart. This paradigm is for the pronoun *I*. [1]

ἐγώ	I	N	ἡμεῖς	we
μου	of me (my)	G	ἡμῶν	of us (our)
μοι	to me	D	ἡμῖν	to us
με	me	A	ἡμᾶς	us

This chart shows us how the pronoun looks wherever it is used in a sentence. We will be memorizing the chart, and trying to use these words in some of our translations. Read through the paradigm several times before beginning your workbook exercises.

day 3: Translating the personal pronoun

Today you will translate first person pronouns from English to Greek. Take special care to select the correct case and number.

---

[1] There are also emphatic forms for the genitive, dative, and accusative singular pronouns. These forms would be used for extra emphasis, and are also often used after prepositions. They are ἐμοῦ, ἐμοί, and ἐμέ.

day 4: Translate from Greek to English

Translate sentences including the first person personal pronoun from Greek into English. Above each word, indicate whether it is a:

subject (S)
verb (V)
direct object (DO)
adjective (adj)
preposition (prep)
object of the preposition (OP)
article (art)
adverb (adv)
pronoun (pro)

day 5: Review vocabulary

14

Personal Pronouns continued

OBJECTIVE:
To continue using the first person personal pronoun.

Memory Verse:

Ἡ χάρις μετὰ πάντων ὑμῶν. Ἀμήν.

(The) grace   (be) with   all   of you.   Amen.

ΠΡΟΣ ΤΙΤΟΝ 3·15
(To)Titus 3:15

day 1 : Vocabulary

Review past Bible verses.

ἡ γῆ	the earth
ἡ συναγωγή	the synagogue
ἡ ἐξουσία	the power
τό σημεῖον	the sign
ἡ σοφία	the wisdom

Notice that all your vocabulary words this week are nouns. What declension are they part of? Are they masculine, feminine, or neuter? How do you know?

You have likely heard the feminine name Sophia. Did you know that it came from the Greek word for wisdom? We have many other words which share a root with the Greek σοφία, such as *sophisticate, sophomore,* and *sophism.* Also, our suffix –sophy, found in words like *philosophy (love+knowledge),* is a derivative of the Greek as well.

Review vocabulary:

πιστός	faithful
πρῶτος	first
ἅγιος	holy
πονηρός	evil
μικρός	small, little

day 2: Memorize personal pronoun declension

Last week you learned how to decline the personal pronoun 'I'. This week we will continue using this pronoun in our translation, but first we need to focus on memorizing the declension for 'I'. Let's start by reading over the paradigm several times. It can be found in last week's lesson.

Once you have read this over several times, move on to your workbook exercises. Try to write as much as you can of the paradigm for the pronoun 'I' without looking at the chart. You will continue writing out this paradigm each day this week to help you commit it to memory.

day 3: Using personal pronouns with prepositions

A preposition is a joining word. You have learned that it joins a noun to a sentence by showing the relationship between the noun and the sentence. A preposition can just as easily join a pronoun to a sentence. We can say *about me, against us, from me*, and so on. When you learned your prepositions, you learned that they require their object to be in a specific case. When the object is a pronoun, you will still have to be careful that you put it in the proper case. Remember that prepositions need objects in the genitive, accusative, or dative cases. The genitive, accusative, and dative singular cases for the pronoun *I* have special forms when they come after a preposition. These forms are called the emphatic forms. To make these pronouns emphatic, we add an epsilon to the beginning of the word and an accent. Because these accents never change, you should memorize how they look on the emphatic forms. Try to remember to use them when you translate these words from English into Greek. The emphatic forms look like this: ἐμοῦ, ἐμοῖ. ἐμέ. When the final letter of a preposition is a vowel, it slides away (the term for this is elision) when the next word also begins with a vowel. Study these examples:

κατ' ἐμοῦ	against me	ἀπ' ἐμοῦ	from me
μετ' ἐμοῖ	with me	ἐν ἡμῖν	in us

ὑπ’ ἐμέ   under me   ὑπερ ἡμᾶς   above us.

Here are two additional instances where the final letter of the preposition changes because the pronoun begins with a vowel. Study these:

μεθ’ ἡμῶν   with us   ἐξ ἡμῶν   out of us

You have seen ἐκ change to ἐξ before other vowels, but you haven't seen this form of μετά before. Notice that two changes have taken place with this word. First, the final alpha slipped away, and then the tau changed to a theta. The tau only changes to a theta when the next word begins with a rough breathing mark. This happens with a few other prepositions as well (κατά becomes καθ’, ἀπό becomes ἀφ’...), but you don't need to memorize all the changes at this point. In general, a tau will become a theta and a pi will become a phi before a rough breathing mark.

day 4: Translate from Greek to English

Today you will classify and translate sentences including the first person personal pronoun in its standard and emphatic forms.

day 5: Review vocabulary

15

Review

OBJECTIVE : Continue learning about the
genitive case, including translation of sentences.

day 1 : Vocabulary and Bible verse review

Begin by reciting Luke 2:14 and Titus 3:15. You should have both of these verses completely memorized.

Vocabulary:

ἄρχω	I rule
ἀναβαίνω	I go up
καταβαίνω	I go down
αἴρω	I take up, I take away
ἐσθίω	I eat
κηρύσσω	I preach
πείθω	I persuade
ἡ φυλακή	the prison
ἡ δικαιοσύνη	the righteousness
οὐ	not
ἐγώ	I
σύ	you
ἀμήν	verily, truly, amen
μόνος	alone, only
ὁ χρόνος	the time
ἡ γῆ	the earth
ἡ συναγωγή	the synagogue
ἡ ἐξουσία	the power
τό σημεῖον	the sign
ἡ σοφία	the wisdom

Quiz yourself on the words above. Spend extra time studying any that you didn't remember.

day 2: Defining personal pronouns

Over the past few weeks, we have been learning about personal pronouns. Pronouns are the little words like *I*, *you*, and *he* that stand in place of nouns (names for people, places, things, or ideas). Like nouns, pronouns have case and number.

So far, we have only been learning how to use the pronoun *I* in its various forms. In a few weeks, we will be looking at the pronoun *you*.

We also have learned recently how to use the adverb *not*. Do you recall the three forms of the word and when to use them?

day 3: Translate from Greek to English

When you translate today's sentences from Greek into English, watch for pronouns and the word *not*...

day 4: Translate from English to Greek

As you translate today's sentences from English to Greek, be sure to use the correct case for the prepositions in these sentences. Classify the words in the sentences by marking:

subject (S)

verb (V)

direct object (DO)

adjective (adj)

preposition (prep)

object of the preposition (OP)

article (art)

adverb (adv)

pronoun (pro)

day 5: Review vocabulary

Read the following paragraph and answer the questions in English.

ὁ ἄνθρωπος ἐν τῇ φυλακῇ κηρύσσει περὶ τῆς δικαιοσύνης τοῦ θεοῦ. ἄνθρωπος λέγει, οἱ πιστοὶ ἄνθρωποι ἔχουσι τὴν σοφίαν ἐν ταῖς καρδίαις αὐτῶν.[1] ὁ ἅγιος ἄνθρωπος πείθει Φαρισαῖον μετὰ λόγων καὶ σημείων. ἡ ἐξουσία τοῦ ἀνθρώπου ἐστί παρὰ τοῦ θεοῦ.

Where is the man who preaches?

What do faithful men have in their hearts?

How does the man persuade the Pharisee?

Where does the man get his power?

---

1 αὐτῶν means *of them/their*

16

Conjunctions

OBJECTIVE:
To learn how to correctly use some of the Greek conjunctions

Ἡμεῖς ἀγαπῶμεν αὐτὸν

We   *love*   *Him*

ΙΩΑΝΝΟΥ Α 4:19
I John 4:19a

This is the first part of I John 4:19, which we will finish memorizing next week. Notice that the first word in this verse is one of the pronouns that you learned in the ἐγω paradigm. What case is the word ἡμεῖς, and what part does it play in the verse above?

day 1 : Vocabulary

Review Bible verses.

ἀλλά	but
εἰ	if
ὅτι	because, that
+δέ	and, but

The first thing you probably noticed about your vocabulary words today is that peculiar 'plus sign' before the Greek word δέ. This sign is present to make us aware that this word cannot ever begin a phrase in Greek, although we commonly begin phrases in English with both the words 'and' and 'but'. This word is referred to grammatically as a postpositive. Usually, it is the second word in the phrase. Notice also that there are two words for 'but' on your list. The word ἀλλά is a strong word, and it is used when you really want to draw attention to the contrast between two things. "I thought he was lying *but* I was wrong." The word δέ is milder: "I thought about going, but decided against it."

You will notice that the word for *if* is nearly identical to the second person singular form of εἰμί, εἶ. The only difference between these two words is that εἰ (if) has no accent, while εἶ (you are) has the circumflex accent. Though you are not required to learn the accents at this point, it is important to note this distinction and remember it.

All of the vocabulary words this week are *conjunctions*. They are words used to join two phrases, words, or thoughts, and they show the relationship between the two parts.

Review vocabulary:

ἀγαθός	good (moral)
ἄλλος	other
ἔσχατος	last
κακός	bad
καλός	good, beautiful

day 2: Using the postpositive δέ

Remember that whenever the word δέ shows up in a sentence or phrase, it is not going to be the lead word like it is in English. Greek writers usually like to slip it in right after the first word in the sentence, regardless of what that word is. Study these examples:

...but the man suffers
ὁ δὲ ἄνθρωπος πάσχει.

...but a faithful apostle speaks
πιστὸς δὲ ἀπόστολος λέγει.

...but I hear
ἀκούω δέ

Notice how the word δέ appears as the second word in each phrase above.

day 3: Translate from Greek to English

The sentences you will be translating today use the conjunctions that were in your vocabulary list. Be sure to keep your eyes open for them, especially the postpositive δέ.

Classify the words as:
subject (S)
verb (V)
direct object (DO)
adjective (adj)
preposition (prep)
object of the preposition (OP)
article (art)
adverb (adv)
pronoun (pro)
conjunction (con)

day 4: Translate from English to Greek

Before you translate today's sentences, take a moment to reread the information from Day 1 regarding your new vocabulary words ἀλλά and δέ.

day 5: Review vocabulary

17

Second Person Personal Pronouns

Ἡμεῖς ἀγαπῶμεν αὐτὸν
We   *love*   *Him*

ὅτι αὐτὸς πρῶτος ἠγάπησεν ἡμᾶς.
because   *He*   *first*   *loved*   *us.*

ΙΩΑΝΝΟΥ Α 4:19
I John 4:19

Notice the word ὅτι, which was one of your vocabulary words last week. Also, notice the personal pronouns in the verse. What case is the word ἡμᾶς in? Do you know why this case is used?

day 1 : Vocabulary

Review past Bible verses.

ἀνοίγω	I open
ἐλέγχω	I rebuke
σπείρω	I sow
παραλαμβάνω	I receive
πάλιν	again

When you pronounce the word ἐλέγχω, are you remembering that the gamma before the chi will say /ng/ ? Say *e LENG cho*.

When we use παρα as a prefix for the verb λαμβάνω, we change the meaning of the verb from take to receive. Notice that the last word on your vocabulary list is an adverb. Adverbs in Greek are constant; their form does not change when used in a sentence. So, again and again and again (πάλιν καὶ πάλιν καὶ πάλιν...) you can use this word without worrying whether it is conjugated or declined correctly! The rest of the words in this list are verbs, which means that they must be conjugated to be used correctly in a sentence.

Review vocabulary:

ἐγώ	I
καλύπτω	I hide
ἡ οἰκία	the house
ὁ καρπός	the fruit
ὁ Χριστός	the Messiah, Christ

day 2 : Declension for personal pronoun *you*

A few lessons ago, you learned the paradigm for the personal pronoun *I*. It is now time to learn a similar paradigm, this time for the pronoun *you*. Pay attention to the similarities between these two paradigms—they will only make this new paradigm easier to learn.

	singular				*plural*	
ἐγώ	I	N		ἡμεῖς	we	
μου	of me (my)	G		ἡμων	of us (our)	
μοι	to me	D		ἡμῖν	to us	
με	me	A		ἡμᾶς	us	

	singular				*plural*	
σύ	you	N		ὑμεῖς	you	
σοῦ	of you (your)	G		ὑμων	of you (your)	
σοί	to you	D		ὑμῖν	to you	
σέ	you	A		ὑμᾶς	you	

As you can see, these paradigms are nearly identical. Refer to them as needed to translate the phrases in today's workbook exercises.

day 3: Translate from Greek to English

As you classify and translate sentences today, remember that πάλιν is an adverb

day 4: Translate from English to Greek

What part of speech is the word *again*?

day 5: Review vocabulary

18

The Dative Case

OBJECTIVE:
To begin learning the proper use of the dative case.

Memory Verse:

Χαίρετε ἐν Κυρίῳ πάντοτε.
Rejoice   in (the) Lord   always.

ΠΡΟΣ ΦΙΛΙΠΠΗΣΙΟΥΣ 4:4
To (the) Phillipians 4:4a

Last year you learned a verse from I Thessalonians which was very similar to this verse. You will notice that this verse expands slightly on last year's "Rejoice always." The word πάντοτε is actually a compound word, made up of the word πάν, meaning every, and the word τότε, meaning then. Rejoice then, and then, and then…rejoice in *every* then…rejoice always.

day 1 : Vocabulary

Review past Bible verses

τό πρόβατον	the sheep
ὁ ἥλιος	the sun
ʼΑβραάμ	Abraham
ὁ δῆμος	the people
ὁ γάμος	the wedding

This week you are learning the Greek word for sun. Perhaps you have learned about *helium* in your science class. Helium, a gas which was first noticed in the sun's atmosphere, was named after the sun. We have many other words which use the prefix helio-, derived from this Greek word. A *helioscope* is an instrument for viewing the sun, *heliocentric* describes our universe, with the sun at its center, and a *heliograph* is an instrument used to photograph the sun. The word δῆμος also has English derivatives in *democracy* (rule by the people) and other words using the demo- prefix. And then there are the words *monogamy* (single marriage) and *polygamy* (having more than one husband/wife), derived from γάμος.

Review vocabulary:

ἡ ἐπαγγελία	the promise
ἡ χαρά	the joy
θέλω	I wish
ἁμαρτάνω	I sin
ὁ Ἰουδαῖος	the Jew

day 2: Identifying the primary use of the dative case

You have learned how to use the nominative case for subjects and predicate nominatives in your sentences. The genitive case is commonly used to show possession, and the accusative case is used for direct objects. Although you have used the dative case as the object of some of the prepositions you have studied, you have not yet learned the primary function of the dative case. That is what we will be learning in this lesson. The dative case is generally associated with the English prepositions *to* and *for*, so we can think of the dative case as the *to/for* case. Just as the genitive case requires the use of the word *of* (or the apostrophe-s), the dative case requires the use of either *to* or *for*.[1]

In these sentences, identify the subject, verb, possessive phrases, direct objects, and prepositional phrases using *to* and *for*.

The young men gave the book to the old men.

The man's children ate bread and jam.

The child throws the ball to the dog.

We take food to the blind men.

---

1 In English, we have many separate meanings for our little word *to*. It is important to remember that not all of these uses are translated the same way into other languages. Although the dative case is used in Greek to show the relationship for which we in English use the indirect object or *to*, its application does not also widen to include all other uses of this word. For example, when to preposition *to* is used to indicate motion toward something, the Greek requires the use of a separate preposition (πρός or ἐπί with the accusative).

day 3: Parsing nouns

Remember that when you see the dative case in Greek, it will require you to use a prepositional phrase in English beginning with either *to* or *for*. Today's workbook exercise includes a list of words to be parsed (gender, number, and case) and translated. In your translation, you can now reflect the case of the noun. For example, the word ἀληθείας (genitive) should be translated *of truth*, and the word ἀληθείᾳ should be translated *to/for truth*.

day 4: Translate from Greek to English

Today you will translate sentences from Greek to English. When you classify, mark nouns in the dative case with a "Dat" and remember to translate them with "to" or "for". Next week we will learn more about the dative case and the name for the job nouns in the dative case perform in a sentence.

day 5: Review vocabulary.

19

The Dative Case

OBJECTIVE: To continue using the dative case in sentences

Memory Verse:

Χαίρετε ἐν Κυρίῳ πάντοτε.
Rejoice   in (the) Lord   always.

Πάλιν ἐρῶ, χαίρετε !
Again   I say,   rejoice!

ΠΡΟΣ ΦΙΛΙΠΠΗΣΙΟΥΣ 4:4
To (the) Phillipians 4:4

day 1 : Vocabulary

Review Bible verses.

ἡ μαρτυρία	the testimony
ὁ ὀφθαλμός	the eye
τό στάδιον	the stadium
ἡ κώμη	the village
ἡ σωτηρία	the salvation

We call an eye doctor an *ophthalmogist*, from the Greek word for eye. A *martyr* is one who suffers because of his Christian testimony (μαρτυρία). Our word *stadium* comes from the Greek στάδιον.

Review vocabulary:

ἡ φωνή	the voice
ἡ ψυχή	the soul, life
ἡ καρδία	the heart
ἡ ἀγάπη	the love
ἡ ἁμαρτία	the sin

day 2: The Indirect Object

In English, we sometimes use indirect objects in our sentences. An indirect object can always be rewritten as a prepositional phrase beginning with "to" or "for". The sentence "The man gave me the ball" has the word 'me' as an indirect object. This sentence could be rewritten "The man gave the ball to me." In either sentence, the word me would be translated into the dative in Greek. Be sure to watch your sentences for indirect objects and prepositional phrases beginning with to/for, both of which will be translated using the dative case.

day 3: Translate from Greek to English

When you classify sentences today, mark nouns in the dative case with "IO" for "indirect object". Remember to translate them with the prepositions "to" or "for".

day 4: Translate from English to Greek

When you classify sentences today, mark nouns in the dative case with "Dat" for "dative case". Which case will you use when you translate indirect objects?

day 5: Review vocabulary.

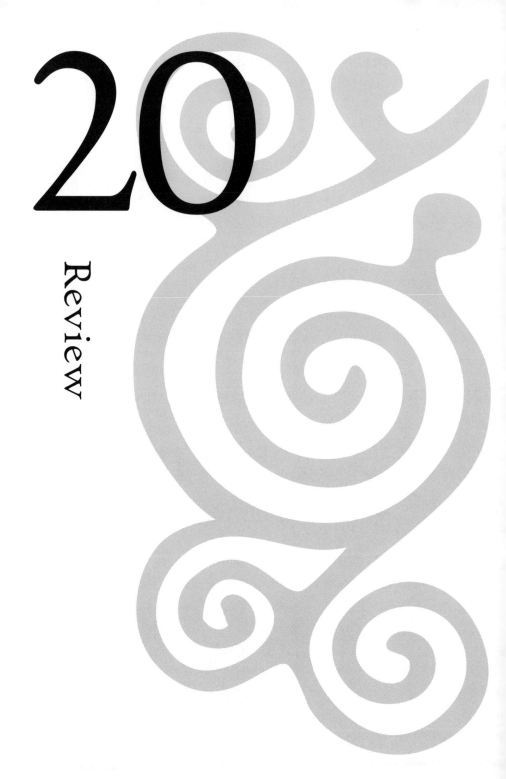

20

Review

OBJECTIVE: To review material covered in the last five weeks

day 1: Review Bible verses. You should be able to recite and give the English translations for I John 4:19 and Philippians 4:4

Vocabulary:

ἀλλά	but
εἰ	if
ὅτι	because, that
+δέ	and, but
ἀνοίγω	I open
ἐλέγχω	I rebuke
σπείρω	I sow
παραλαμβάνω	I receive
πάλιν	again
τό πρόβατον	the sheep
ὁ ἥλιος	the sun
Ἀβραάμ	Abraham
ὁ δῆμος	the people
ὁ γάμος	the wedding
ἡ μαρτυρία	the testimony
ὁ οφθαλμός	the eye
τό στάδιον	the stadium
ἡ κώμη	the village
ἡ σωτηρία	the salvation

Quiz yourself on these words. Spend the week reviewing any that you were unable to translate.

day 2: Recognizing conjunctions and reviewing the word 'not'

A few weeks ago, we began using conjunctions in our sentences. Remember that a conjunction is a joining word. We use conjunctions to join words, phrases, or sentences. Most of the conjunctions that we learned are used much like their English equivalents, but we did have one word, called a postpositive, which follows some specific rules about placement in the sentence/phrase. Do you remember what is special about a postpositive?

You have also learned about the adverb 'not'. Recall that there are three forms, to be used according to the first letter of the next word. Which form is used before consonants? Which before vowels with a rough breathing mark?

day 3: Parsing nouns

You are now able to use each of the cases in their primary uses. There are still many things to learn about the different cases, but for now you have an excellent start on translation work, because you know how each case is usually used. Regularly review the primary uses, to be sure that you remember the case and its use.

Nominative   subject
Genitive   of a (possessive)
Dative   to/for (indirect object)
Accusative   direct object

day 4: Identifying pronouns

Here is a portion of the Lord's prayer, which is found in Matthew 6. Read through it carefully, paying attention to the words and forms you have learned. With a little practice, you should be able to read through the whole prayer smoothly.

Πάτερ ἡμῶν ὁ ἐν τοῖς οὐρανοῖς,
Our father in heaven,

ἁγιασθήτω τὸ ὄνομα σου,
Hallowed be your name,

ἐλθέτω ἡ βασιλεία σου,
Your kingdom come,

γενηθήτω τό θέλημά σου,
Your will be done,

ὡς ἐν οὐρανῷ καὶ ἐπὶ τῆς γῆς.
On earth as it is in heaven.

τὸν ἄρτον ἡμῶν τὸν επιούσιον δὸς ἡμῖν σήμερον.
Give us this day our daily bread.

καὶ ἄφες ἡμῖν τὰ ὀφειλήματα ἡμῶν,
And forgive us our debts,

ὡς καὶ ἡμεῖς ἀφίεμεν τοῖς ὀφειλέταις ἡμῶν,
As we forgive our debtors,

day 5: Review vocabulary

21

The Imperfect Tense

OBJECTIVE:
To begin learning the imperfect active indicative tense endings

Memory Verse:

Ἡ σωτηρία τῷ Θεῷ ἡμῶν

ΑΠΟΚΑΛΥΨΙΣ 7:10
Revelation 7:10

You will notice that I have not provided the translation for your new verse. If I tell you that the word *belongs* is implied between σωτηρία and τῷ Θεῷ, you should be able to translate this passage on your own. See now how many words you know before looking at the word-for-word translation in the footnote.[1] Notice also that the Greek name for Revelation is ἀποκάλυψις. This word is transliterated into English as "Apocalypse," and the book of Revelation is sometimes called The Apocalypse.

day 1 : Vocabulary

Review Bible verses.

θεραπεύω	I heal
διώκω	I persecute
εὑρίσκω	I find
ὁ θρόνος	the throne
κόπτω	I cut

Do you remember reading about Archimedes in your history class? Archimedes was trying to find the answer to a problem. The king had asked him to figure out if his crown was made out of pure gold. Archimedes was thinking about this problem while he bathed one day. When the answer occurred to him, he jumped out of his bath, and ran down the street shouting, "Eureka!", or "I found it!" We still say "eureka" today when we are excited about finding something. Eureka is also the motto of the state of California. Can you think of why this would be? Eureka comes from your vocabulary word εὑρίσκω.

---

1 The salvation *belongs* to the God of us (or, Salvation belongs to our God.)

Review vocabulary:

ἡ γραφή	the writing, Scripture
ἡ παραβολή	the parable
ἡ εἰρήνη	the peace
ἡ ἐντολή	the commandment
ἡ ζωή	the life

day 2: Recognizing the imperfect tense

This week we will begin learning about a new tense for our verbs. We already know how to conjugate verbs in the present tense. The present tense is used for an action that is happening right now. "I find" is in the present tense. "I do find," and "I am finding," are also in the present tense. If you say "I find," you are talking about something you are doing right now. "I found" is in the past tense. We use the past tense to talk about something we have already done. If I say "I found" I am talking about something I have completed. But we are going to learn the endings for the *imperfect tense*. The imperfect tense is used to talk about something we kept on doing in the past. If you say, "I was finding" you are talking about something you kept doing in the past…something that took you a long time to do. We say that the imperfect tense is used to show continuous action in the past. We always translate it into English using the helping verb was/were.

She was jumping.
You were talking.
They were cutting.
I was walking.

day 3: The imperfect tense paradigm

In Greek, the imperfect tense is formed differently than the present tense is. The first thing to remember is that in the imperfect tense, the letter epsilon is added onto the beginning of the stem. This is called an *augment*. Then, the actual endings are different. Here is λύω in the imperfect tense.

ἔλυον   ἐλύομεν
ἔλυες   ἐλύετε
ἔλυε   ἔλυον

If λύω means "I loose", then ἔλυον means "I was loosing". Thus:

I was loosing   we were loosing
you were loosing   you were loosing
he, she, or it was loosing   they were loosing

Say the conjugation a few times through until you are familiar with it. How is the beginning of the verb λύω different when it is in the imperfect tense?

day 4: Translating verbs

Sometimes the word ἔλυε (he was loosing) looks a little different when it is used in a sentence. A third person singular verb in the imperfect tense takes a movable nu if the next word in the sentence begins with a vowel or if it is the last word in the sentence. So, ἔλυε changes to ἔλυεν. Remember that you have seen this from time to time on your present tense verbs. It should remind you of the *n* we add to the article *a* before words beginning with a vowel (*an iceberg, an owl, an apple*).

day 5: Review vocabulary

22

The Imperfect Tense, continued

OBJECTIVE: To continue working
with the imperfect active indicative tense endings.

Memory Verse:

Ἡ σωτηρία τῷ Θεῷ ἡμῶν
The   salvation   (belongs) to the God   of us

Τῷ καθημένῳ ἐπὶ τῷ θρόνῳ
To the (One)   sitting   on   the   throne

ΑΠΟΚΑΛΥΨΙΣ 7·10
Revelation 7:10

The word *throne* should be familiar to you. That leaves only καθημένῳ and ἐπὶ
as unfamiliar words in this verse. καθημένῳ is a participle form of the verb
which means 'to sit'. A participle is a verb acting as an adjective. Hear, the word
sitting is used to describe *the One* (God). ἐπὶ is a preposition taking the dative.

day 1 : Vocabulary

Review Bible verses.

ἀντί (with genitive)	instead of
ἀποθνήσκω	I die
ἀποκτείνω	I kill
ἡ Γαλιλαία	Galilee
δοξάζω	I glorify

Perhaps you sing the doxology as part of your church service. The word *doxology*
means to speak glory or praise (specifically to God) and as you can see it is a
derivative from the Greek.

Review vocabulary:

ἡ ἀλήθεια	the truth
ἡ βασιλεία	the kingdom
ἡ ἐκκλησία	the church

ἡ ἡμέρα	the day
ἡ ὥρα	the hour

day 2: Conjugating verbs in the imperfect tense

Last week we began learning how to conjugate a verb in the imperfect tense. In English, the imperfect tense uses the helping verb *was/were*. In Greek, the imperfect tense doesn't use a helping verb, but it has its own set of personal endings, which are different than the present tense endings. It also has an augment, which is a letter added onto the **beginning** of the stem.

Here is a chart for λύω in the imperfect tense.

ἔλυον	I was loosing	ἐλύομεν	we were loosing
ἔλυες	you were loosing	ἐλύετε	you were loosing
ἔλυε(ν)	he was loosing	ἔλυον	they were loosing

day 3: Changes to the augment in the imperfect tense

Sometimes a verb will begin with an alpha or an epsilon. When we want to conjugate one of these verbs in the imperfect tense, we must follow a special rule. This rule is: **When the verb begins with a vowel (α, ε) the vowel is lengthened (η) to show that the augment has been added.** If the verb begins with alpha or epsilon, it will begin with an eta when the verb is put into the imperfect tense.

ε + ἀκούω = εακουον = ἤκουον   I was hearing

ε + ἔχω = εεχον = ἤχον   I was holding

day 4: Translate from Greek to English

When you translate today's sentences, pay special attention to verb tenses.

day 5: Review vocabulary

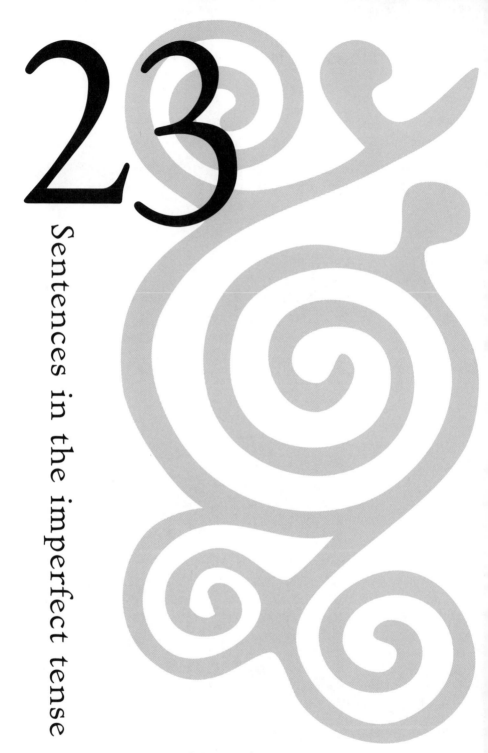

23

Sentences in the imperfect tense

OBJECTIVE:
To begin translating sentences using the imperfect tense

Memory Verse:

Ἡ σωτηρία   τῷ Θεῷ ἡμῶν
The   salvation (belongs) to   the God   of us

Τῷ καθημένῳ ἐπὶ τῷ θρόνῳ,
To the (One)   sitting   on   the   throne,

Καὶ τῷ Ἀρνίῳ
And to the   Lamb

ΑΠΟΚΑΛΥΨΙΣ 7·10
Revelation 7:10

day 1 : Vocabulary

Review past Bible verses.

κράζω	I cry out
χαίρω	I rejoice, am glad
ᾄδω	I sing
ὀφείλω	I owe
πίνω	I drink

All of your vocabulary words this week are verbs. You may recognize the word χαίρω from Philippians 4:4, which you memorized several weeks ago. Remember that it was used in its second person plural form: χαίρετε—you rejoice.

Review vocabulary:

ὁ ἄρτος	the bread
σώζω	I save
βαίνω	I go
ὁ τυφλός	the blind man
Ἰησοῦς	Jesus

day 2: Adding the augment to compound verbs

We have already learned that the augment goes immediately before the stem when the verb is in the imperfect tense. You practiced adding the augment in the conjugations you did above. However, some of the verbs you have learned this year are compound verbs. The compound verbs you have learned all have prepositional prefixes. When a compound verb is in the imperfect tense, the augment is inserted between the preposition and the verb stem. If the preposition ends with a vowel (as most prepositions do), the vowel is replaced by the augment. In the case of ἐκ, as in ἐκβάλλω, the addition of the augment means that the kappa must be changed to a xi. All of the compound verbs you have learned this year are listed below, along with their imperfect forms.

ἐκβάλλω → ἐξέβαλλον Notice that the κ is changed to a ξ.

ἀναβαίνω → ἀνέβαινον The α is replaced by the augment

καταβαίνω → κατέβαινον The α is replaced by the augment ε.

παραλαμβάνω → παρελάμβανον Again, the augment replaces the α.

ἀποστέλλω → ἀπέστελλον The ο is replaced by the augment ε.

ἀποθνήσκω → ἀπέθνησκον The ο is replaced by the augment ε.

ἀποκτείνω → ἀπέκτεινον The ο is replaced by the augment ε.

day 3: Translate from Greek to English

When you translate today, remember to look for verbs in the imperfect tense. They will be easy to spot, because of the augment or lengthened vowel which will precede the verb stem.

day 4 : Translate from English to Greek

Today you will classify and translate sentences from English to Greek. Remember that the helping verb and verb will translate to a single *imperfect tense* form in Greek.

day 5 : Review vocabulary

24

Imperfect of εἰμί

OBJECTIVE: To learn the paradigm for εἰμί in the imperfect tense

Memory Verse:

Ἡ σωτηρία τῷ Θεῷ ἡμῶν
The   salvation (belongs) to the God   of us

Τῷ καθημένῳ ἐπὶ τῷ θρόνῳ,
To the (One)   sitting   on   the   throne,

Καὶ τῷ Ἀρνίῳ
And   to the   Lamb

ΑΠΟΚΑΛΥΨΙΣ 7·10
Revelation 7:10

day 1 : Vocabulary

Review past Bible verses.

ὑπάκούω	I obey
ἡ παρουσία	the presence, coming
ἡ εὐλογία	the praise, blessing
ὁ γεωργός	the farmer
γνωρίζω	I reveal

Last week you learned that a compound verb in the imperfect tense takes the augment between the prefix and the stem. Your first vocabulary word this week is a compound verb. Can you identify the stem and the prefix? The stem is already familiar to you in the form of the verb ακούω, I hear. You have also seen the prefix, ὑπό, before. It is possible that you didn't recognize ὑπό because it is missing its final letter in the word above. When a prefix ending with a vowel is attached to a verb beginning with a vowel, the final letter of the prefix is dropped. That means that when you put this verb in the imperfect tense, part of your work is already done for you. You only need to lengthen the first letter of the stem and use the imperfect ending to get ὑπήκουον, I was obeying.

Note that εὐλογία shares a stem with λόγος, *word*. In English, the word *eulogy* refers to a commendation of a person or thing. At funerals, a eulogy is often given.

The word γνωρίζω also shares a stem with another Greek word you have already studied. Last year, you learned that γινώσκω means *I know*.

Review vocabulary:

τό βιβλίον	the book
τό δαιμόνιον	the demon
τό ἔργον	the work
τό πλοῖον	the boat
ὁ ἁμαρτωλός	the sinner

day 2: The imperfect of εἰμί

Over the past few weeks, you have learned many things about conjugating verbs in the imperfect tense. This week, we have one more thing to learn. Last year, we studied the irregular verb εἰμί in the present tense. Because of this, we can say things like "The man *is* an apostle." and "God *is* good." Now, we are going to learn how to conjugate this same verb in the imperfect tense. We will be able to say "The men *were* evil." and "The children *were* sons of the blind man."

The imperfect of εἰμί:

ἤμην	I was	ἦμεν	we were
ἦς	you were	ἦτε	you were
ἦν	he was	ἦσαν	they were

Read through the paradigm a few times until you feel comfortable with it.

Usually when you see this verb used in sentences, it will be a linking verb. This means that it will link either a predicate nominative or a predicate adjective to the subject of the sentence. Remember that the predicate nominative/adjective will be in the same case as the subject—the nominative case.

day 3 : Translate from Greek to English

Today you will classify and translate sentences using the imperfect form of εἰμί.

day 4 : Translate from English to Greek

Today you will classify and translate sentences into Greek. You may refer to your paradigm for the imperfect form of εἰμί if necessary, but continue to review the forms daily and work toward memorizing them completely.

day 5 : Review vocabulary

25

Review

OBJECTIVE : To review information from the last five lessons

day 1 : Review Bible verses. You should be able to recite Revelation 7:10

Vocabulary:

θεραπεύω	I heal
διώκω	I persecute
εὑρίσκω	I find
ὁ θρόνος	the throne
κόπτω	I cut
ἀντί (with the genitive)	instead of
ἀποθνήσκω	I die
ἀποκτείνω	I kill
ἡ Γαλιλαία	Galilee
δοξάζω	I glorify
κράζω	I cry out
χαίρω	I rejoice, am glad
ᾄδω	I sing
ὀφείλω	I owe
πίνω	I drink
ὑπακούω	I obey
ἡ παρουσία	the presence, coming
ἡ εὐλογία	the praise, blessing
ὁ γεωργός	the farmer
γνωρίζω	I reveal

Quiz yourself on these words. Spend the week reviewing any that you were unable to translate.

day 2 : Translating verbs

You have spent the last few weeks learning about the imperfect tense. This tense is easy to recognize because of the augment which precedes the verb stem. Remember that in English it is necessary to use the helping verb was/were to correctly convey the meaning of the imperfect tense.

day 3: Translate verbs into Greek

Today you will translate verbs into Greek. Pay special attentiont to tense!

day 4: Translate from Greek to English

Today you will translate sentences in both the present and imperfect tense.

day 5: Review vocabulary

Read the following paragraph and answer the questions in English.

ἐστὶ παραβολή περὶ πρόβατον. τὸ πρόβατον οὐκ ἦν ἐν τῷ ἀγρῷ. ὁ γεωργὸς οὐκ ἔβλεπε τὸ πρόβατον. ὁ γεωργὸς ἔκραζω ἐν τοῖς ἀγροῖς καὶ ἐν ταῖς κώμαις. ὁ γεωργὸς εὑρίσκει τὸ πρόβατον. χαίρει.

What is this parable about?

What has the farmer lost?

Where does the farmer call for the sheep?

What does the farmer do when he finds the sheep?

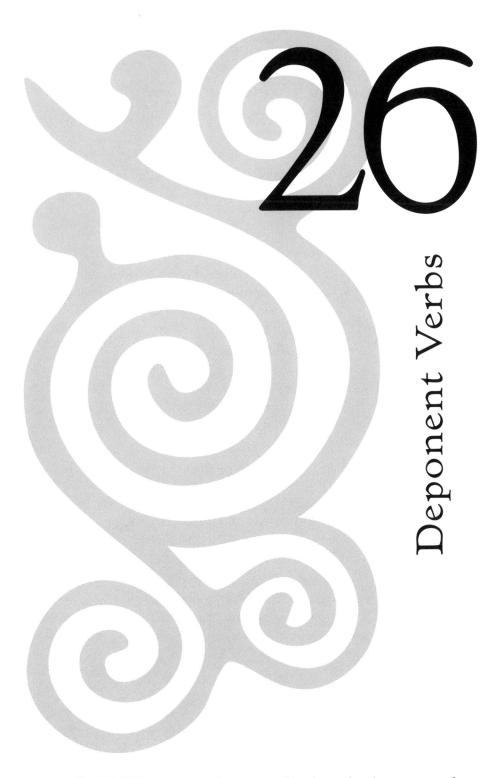

26

Deponent Verbs

OBJECTIVE: To learn the personal endings for deponent verbs

Memory Verse:

Ἐγω εἰμι ἡ ἄμπελος ἡ ἀληθινή
I   am   the   vine   the   true

ΚΑΤΑ ΙΩΑΝΝΗΝ 15:1
(According to) John 15:1

English translations usually read:
I am the true vine

day 1: Vocabulary

Review past Bible verses.

γίνομαι	I become
ἀποκρίνομαι	I answer (takes the dative)
ἄρχομαι	I begin
δέχομαι	I receive
ἔρχομαι	I come, I go

Notice that these words are all verbs, but they do not end with the omega, as you are accustomed to seeing. These words are called **deponent verbs**, and they use a different set of endings.[1] They are still translated in the present tense. Especially notice the verb ἀποκρίνομαι above. In your vocabulary list, it says that this word takes the dative. That means that the direct object which comes after "I answer…" is actually in the dative case, instead of in the accusative case like most direct objects.

I answer the man.
ἀποκρίνομαι τῷ ἀνθρώπῳ.

---

1 Deponent endings are actually borrowed endings. In Greek, there are three voices: the active, middle, and passive. All verbs have a *voice*, and all the voices have their own endings. Because you are only learning about *active* verbs, you haven't learned any of the other voice endings. Deponent verbs are active verbs that borrow the middle/passive voice endings.

I answer the child.
ἀποκρίνομαι τῷ τέκνῳ.

Notice that the words for child and man in the sentences above are both in the dative case.

Review vocabulary:

τό τέκνον	the child
τό εὐαγγέλιον	the gospel
τό πρόσωπον	the face
τό ἱερόν	the temple
τό δῶρον	the gift

day 2: The deponent endings

In your workbook you will review the regular endings for verbs in the present and imperfect tenses. Now you will learn the deponent endings for verbs in the present tense. To find the stem of the vocabulary words above, we must remove the –ομαι, which is the first person singular (I) ending. Then you add the endings in the chart below onto the stem.

Singular			Plural	
–ομαι	I	*first person*	–ομεθα	we
–η	you	*second person*	–εσθε	you
–εται	he	*third person*	–ονται	they

A conjugated verb will look like this:

γίνομαι	γινόμεθα
γίνη	γίνεσθε
γίνεται	γίνονται

Can you fill in the English translations for the chart above?

Now try to orally conjugate δέχομαι and ἔρχομαι.

day 3: Translating verbs

Today you will translate deponent verbs into English. Be sure to pay attention to endings, and translate correctly.

day 4: Translating verbs into Greek

When you translate from English into Greek today, remember to use the correct deponent endings.

day 5: Review vocabulary

27

Deponent Verbs

Memory Verse:

"Ἐγὼ εἰμι ἡ ἄμπελος ἡ ἀληθινή,
I   am   the   vine   the   true,

καὶ ὁ Πατήρ μου ὁ γεωργός ἐστι.
And   the Father   of me   the farmer   is.

KATA ΙΩΑΝΝΗΝ 15:1
(According to) John 15:1

Your English Bible will say something like:
I am the true vine, and my Father is the vinedresser.

day 1 : Vocabulary

Review past Bible verses.

λογίζομαι	I think
εὐαγγελίζομαι	I preach
ἐργάζομαι	I work
χαρίζομαι	I forgive
βούλομαι	I wish, desire

Notice that your vocabulary words this week are once again deponent verbs. These verbs are translated into English in the present active tense. Almost all of these words should look familiar to you, because you have learned other words that share roots with the ones above. λογίζομαι/ λόγος, εὐαγγελίζομαι/ εὐαγγελιον, ἐργάζομαι/ ἐργον.

Review vocabulary:

πέμπω	I send
φέρω	I bear, bring
βαπτίζω	I baptize

| κρίνω | I judge |
| ὁ διδάσκαλος | the teacher |

day 2: Translating verbs

Today you will translate verbs into English. Notice that there are regular and deponent present tense verbs as well as imperfect tense verbs in the exercise.

day 3: Translate sentences from Greek to English

Today you will classify and translate sentences from Greek to English.

day 4: Translate sentences into Greek

Classify and translate sentences into Greek.

day 5: Review vocabulary

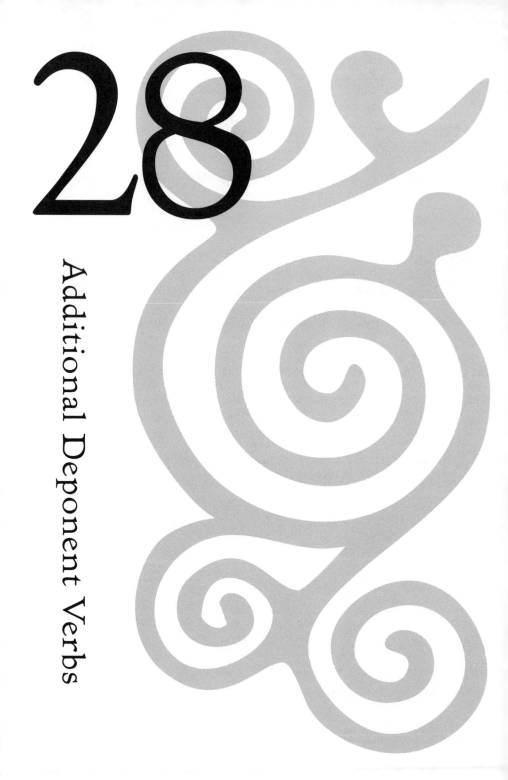

28

Additional Deponent Verbs

OBJECTIVE: To continue using deponent verbs in sentences

Memory Verse:

Ἐγω εἰμι ἡ ἄμπελος,
I   am   the   vine,

ὑμεῖς τὰ κλήματα.
you (are)   the   branches.

KATA ΙΩΑΝΝΗΝ 15:5
(According to) John 15:5

Notice that your Bible verse this week is very similar to the one you learned last week. It begins with the same phrase, "I am the vine..." and is even from the same book and chapter of the Bible.

day 1 : Vocabulary

Review Bible verses.

ἔρχομαι   I come, I go
εἰσέρχομαι   I go in, enter
ἐξέρχομαι   I go out
διέρχομαι   I go through
κἀγώ   and I

You should find your vocabulary list this week to be very simple. As long as you have been reviewing your preposition definitions, you should be able to figure out the meaning of the three words after ἔρχομαι without a problem. Notice that they are simply combinations of the verb "I go" with various prepositions. The word κἀγώ is a contraction of two words: καί and ἐγώ. If you can remember that these common words mean 'and' and 'I', you will have no problems remembering that together they mean 'and I'.

Review vocabulary:

ὁ οὐρανός	the heaven
ὁ τόπος	the place
ἐγείρω	I raise up
ἄγω	I lead
μένω	I remain

day 2 : Translate into Greek

Recall your deponent endings as you translate verbs into Greek today.

day 3 : Translate sentences into English

Classify and translate sentences.

day 4 : Translate sentences into Greek

Classify and translate sentences into Greek. Take care to use the correct tense and endings for your verbs, but don't forget that nouns, articles and adjectives need the correct endings as well.

day 5 : Review

29

Masculine Nouns
of the First Declension

Memory Verse:

᾿Εγω εἰμι ἡ ἄμπελος,
I   am   the   vine,

ὑμεῖς τὰ κλήματα.
you (are) the branches.

ΚΑΤΑ ΙΩΑΝΝΗΝ 15:5
(According to) John 15:5

day 1 : Vocabulary

Review Bible verses.

ὁ μαθητής	the disciple
ὁ προφήτης	the prophet
ὁ νεανίας	the young man
νῦν	now
οὔπω	not yet

The first three of your vocabulary words relate directly to this week's lesson: masculine nouns of the first declension. As you can see by the article (ὁ), these words are most definitely masculine. Even in cases where the article is omitted, these words are obviously masculine based on their meaning—they all name specific kids of men. However, the endings on these words reveal that they are not part of the second declension, like all other masculine nouns we have learned (they do not end in –ος). In fact, they are part of the first declension, and you will be spending time in this lesson learning more about them.

The final two words are adverbs. Remember that an adverb modifies a verb. These two adverbs answer the question *when.*

He reads now.
We are not yet going.

I will now sing.
He has not arrived yet.

Review vocabulary:

ὁ θάνατος	the death
ὁ οἶκος	the house
ὁ υἱός	the son
ὁ κύριος	the lord
ὁ λίθος	the stone

day 2: First declension masculine noun paradigm

The masculine first-declension nouns that we looked at yesterday do not use all of the same case endings as the other first declension nouns we have learned so far. Look carefully at the chart for the word προφήτης below.

προφήτης	N	προφῆται
προφήτου	G	προφητῶν
προφήτῃ	D	προφήταις
προφήτην	A	προφήτας

As you can see, there are only two differences between this chart and the first-declension endings you have already learned. The nominative singular form of the word ends in a *sigma*, and the genitive singular ending (–ου) is the standard masculine second-declension ending. The rest of the endings are identical to the first-declension endings you have learned for stems ending in eta.

Now take a look at the paradigm for νεανίας. Perhaps you can even guess what the endings for this word will look like.

νεανίας	N	νεανίαι
νεανίου	G	νεανιῶν

νεανίᾳ	D	νεανίαις
νεανίαν	A	νεανίας

Again, you can see that there are the same two differences...the rest of the paradigm follows the ending for stems ending in alpha.

day 3: Agreement between nouns and adjectives

Because the three nouns you have been studying this week are masculine, you must be careful to use masculine adjectives with them, even though their endings may make you think you should use the feminine forms of the adjectives. It is wrong to say καλὴ προφήτης, because καλή is a feminine form of the adjective *good*. We need to use the masculine form: καλὸς προφήτης. Also, the form of the article *the* must be masculine: ὁ καλὸς προφήτης.

day 4: Translating sentences

Today you will translate sentences including the first declension masculine nouns you have learned about this week. Notice that the adjectives and articles must always agree with the nouns in gender, number and case, but this does not mean that the endings will be identical.

day 5: Review vocabulary

30

Review

OBJECTIVE: To review concepts introduced in lessons 26-29

day 1: Review Bible verses. You should be able to recite John 15:1 and John 15:5.

Vocabulary:

γίνομαι	I become
ἀποκρίνομαι	I answer (takes the dative)
ἄρχομαι	I begin
δέχομαι	I receive
λογίζομαι	I think
εὐαγγελίζομαι	I preach
ἐργάζομαι	I work
χαρίζομαι	I forgive
βούλομαι	I wish, desire
ἔρχομαι	I come, I go
εἰσέρχομαι	I go in, enter
ἐξέρχομαι	I go out
διέρχομαι	I go through
κἀγώ	and I
ὁ μαθητής	the disciple
ὁ προφήτης	the prophet
ὁ νεανίας	the young man
νῦν	now
οὔπω	not yet

Quiz yourself on these words. Spend the week reviewing any that you were unable to translate.

day 2: Deponenet verb endings

You have been learning about the deponent verbs. Remember that the deponent verbs borrow their endings from the middle/passive voice, but they are still translated as present active verbs.

day 3: Declining masculine first declension nouns

You have learned the main characteristics of each noun declension in previous weeks, and last week you learned about some of the less common words in the first declension. Do you remember what was unusual about these words?

The nouns you learned last week were masculine, and part of the first declension. All the other nouns in the first declension that you have learned have been feminine. These masculine nouns had a few variations in the standard first declension endings, also.

day 4: Translating sentences

Today you will translate sentences from Greek into English.

day 5: Review vocabulary

Read the following paragraph and answer the questions in English.

ὁ διδάσκαλος βαπτίζει τὸν υἱὸν τοῦ κυρίου τῆς βασιλείας. ἐστὶ νεανίας ἐστί δὲ πιστός. ὁ κύριος χαίρει μετὰ τοῦ νεανίου. ὁ νεανίας γίνεται μαθητὴς τοῦ Χριστοῦ. λογίζεται περὶ τοῦ θεοῦ νῦν.

Who does the disciple baptize?

What does the father (the lord) do?

What does the young man become?

What does he think about?

Congratulations!

You have completed your second year of Greek study. This year you have learned another 95 vocabulary words, 9 Bible verses, and several more grammatical concepts. You can recognize and use all 4 noun cases in sentences, and you know two more verb conjugations. Well done!

Appendix A: Greek-English Vocabulary Index

Ἀβραάμ	Abraham	
ἀγαθός	good (moral)	*Agatha*
ἀγάπη, ἡ	love	
ἄγγελος, ὁ	messenger, angel	*angel*
ἅγιος	holy	*Hagia Sophia*
ἀγρός, ὁ	field	*agriculture*
ἄγω	I lead	
ἀδελφή, ἡ	sister	
ἀδελφός, ὁ	brother	*Philadelphia*
αἴρω	I take up, I take away	
ἀκούω	I hear	*acoustic*
ἀλήθεια, ἡ	truth	
ἀλλά	but	
ἄλλος	other	*alien*
ᾄδω	I sing	
ἁμαρτάνω	I sin	
ἁμαρτία, ἡ	sin	
ἁμαρτωλός, ὁ	sinner	
ἀμήν	verily, truly, amen	*amen*
ἀναβαίνω	I go up	
ἄνθρωπος, ὁ	man	*anthropology*
ἀνοίγω	I open	
ἀντί (with gen)	instead of	
ἀπό (with gen)	from	*apology*
ἀποθνήσκω	I die	
ἀποκρίνομαι	I answer (takes the dative)	
ἀποκτείνω	I kill	
ἀποστέλλω	I send	
ἀπόστολος, ὁ	apostle	*apostle*
ἄρτος, ὁ	bread	

ἀρχή, ἡ	beginning	*archaic, archeology*
ἄρχομαι	I begin	
ἄρχω	I rule	
βαίνω	I go	
βάλλω	I throw	*ballistic*
βαπτίζω	I baptize	*baptize*
βασιλεία, ἡ	kingdom	*basil, basilica*
βίος, ὁ	life	*biology*
βιβλίον, τό	book	*Bible, bibliography*
βλέπω	I see	
βούλομαι	I wish, desire	
Γαλιλαία	Galilee	
γάμος, ὁ	wedding	*monogamy, polygamy*
γεωργός, ὁ	farmer	*George*
γῆ, ἡ	earth	
γίνομαι	I become	
γινώσκω	I know	*know, Gnostic*
γνωρίζω	I reveal	
γραφη, ἡ	writing, Scripture	*graph, graphic*
γράφω	I write	*graphite*
δαιμόνιον, τό	demon	*demon*
δῆμος, ὁ	people	*democracy*
+δέ	and, but	
δέκα	ten	*decade*
δεύτερος	second	*Deuteronomy*
δέχομαι	I receive	
διά (with gen)	through	*diameter*
διδάσκαλος, ὁ	teacher	
διδάσκω	I teach	*didactic*
διέρχομαι	I go through	
δίκαιος	righteous	
δικαιοσύνη, ἡ	righteousness	

διώκω	I persecute	
δοξάζω	I glorify	
δοῦλος, ὁ	slave	
δῶρον, τό	gift	
ἐγείρω	I raise up	
ἐγώ	I	*ego*
εἰρήνη, ἡ	peace	*Irene, irenic*
εἰ	if	
εἰς (with acc)	into	
εἰσέρχομαι	I go in, enter	
ἐκ/ἐξ(with gen)	out of	*exit*
ἐκβάλλω	I cast out	
ἐκκλησία, ἡ	church	*ecclesiastical*
ἐλέγχω	I rebuke	
ἐν (with dative)	in	
ἐντολή, ἡ	commandment	
ἐξέρχομαι	I go out	
ἐξουσία, ἡ	power	
ἐπαγγελία, ἡ	promise	
ἐργάζομαι	I work	
ἔργον, τό	work	*erg, ergonomic*
ἔρημος, ἡ	desert	*hermit*
ἔρχομαι	I come, I go	
ἐσθίω	I eat	
ἔσχατος	last	*eschatology*
εὐαγγελίζομαι	I preach	
εὐαγγέλιον, τό	gospel	*evangelical*
εὐλογία, ἡ	praise, blessing	*eulogy*
εὑρίσκω	I find	*eureka!*
ἔχω	I have or hold	
ζωή, ἡ	life	*zoo, zoology*
ἥλιος, ὁ	sun	*helium, heliocentric*

ἡμέρα, ἡ	day	
θάνατος, ὁ	death	*Thanatopsis, euthanasia*
θέλω	I wish	
θεός, ὁ	God	*theology*
θεραπεύω	I heal	*therapy, therapeutic*
θρόνος, ὁ	throne	*throne*
θύρα, ἡ	door	
ἱερόν, τό	temple	
Ἰησοῦς	Jesus	
Ἰουδαῖος, ὁ	Jew	
κἀγώ	and I	
καί	and	
κακός	bad	*cacophony*
καλός	good, beautiful	*kaleidoscope*
καλύπτω	I hide	
καρδία, ἡ	heart	*cardiologist*
καρπός, ὁ	fruit	
κατά(with gen)	against	*cataclysm*
καταβαίνω	I go down	
κηρύσσω	I preach	
κόπτω	I cut	
κόσμος, ὁ	world	*cosmos, cosmic*
κράζω	I cry out	
κρίνω	I judge	
κύριος, ὁ	lord	
κώμη, ἡ	village	
λαμβάνω	I take	
λέγω	I say or speak	*legend*
λίθος , ὁ	stone	*lithography, monolith*
λογίζομαι	I think	*logical*
λόγος, ὁ	word	*theology, biology, etc*
λύω	I loose or destroy	

μαθητής, ὁ	disciple	
μαρτυρία, ἡ	testimony	
μένω	I remain	*remain*
μετά(with gen)	with	*metaphor*
μικρός	small, little	*microscope, microbe*
μόνος	alone, only	*monologue, monolith*
νεανίας, ὁ	young man	
νεκρός	dead	*necrosis*
νόμος, ὁ	law	*Deuteronomy*
νῦν	now	
ὁδός, ἡ	road, way	*exodus*
οἰκία , ἡ	house	
οἶκος, ὁ	house	
ὅτι	because, that	
οὐ	not	
οὔπω	not yet	
οὐρανός, ὁ	heaven	*uranium*
ὀφθαλμός, ὁ	eye	
ὀφείλω	I owe	
ὄχλος	crowd	
πάλιν	again	
παρά (with gen)	from	*paramedic*
παραβολη, ἡ	parable	*parable*
παραλαμβάνω	I receive	
παρουσία, ἡ	presence, coming	
πάσχω	I suffer	
πείθω	I persuade	
πέμπω	I send	
περί (with gen)	about	*perimeter*
πέτρα, ἡ	rock	*Peter, petrify*
πίνω	I drink	
πίπτω	I fall	

πιστεύω	I believe	*epistemology*
πιστός	faithful	
πλοῖον, τό	boat	
πονηρός	evil	
πρό (with gen)	before	*prologue*
πρόβατον, τό	sheep	
πρόσωπον, τό	face	
προφήτης, ὁ	prophet	*prophet*
πρῶτος	first	*prototype*
σημεῖον, τό	sign	
σοφία, ἡ	wisdom	*Sophia, sophomore*
σπείρω	I sow	
στάδιον, τό	stadium	
σταυρός, ὁ	cross	
σύ	you	
σύν (with dat)	with	
συναγωγή, ἡ	synagogue	*synagogue*
σώζω	I save	
σωτηρία, ἡ	salvation	*soteriology*
τέκνον, τό	child	
τιμή, ἡ	honor	
τόπος, ὁ	place	*topography, topology*
τυφλός, ὁ	blind man	
υἱός, ὁ	son	
ὑπακούω	I obey	
ὑπέρ (with acc.)	above	*hyperactive*
ὑπό (with acc.)	under	*hypodermic, hypothesis*
Φαρισαῖος, ὁ	Pharisee	*Pharisee*
φέρω	I bear, bring	
φυλακή, ἡ	prison	
φωνή, ἡ	voice	*telephone, phonograph*
χαίρω	I rejoice, am glad	

χαρά , ἡ	joy	*charismatic*
χαρίζομαι	I forgive	
Χριστός, ὁ	Messiah, Christ	*Christ*
χρόνος, ὁ	time	*chronology*
χώρα, ἡ	country	
ψυχή, ἡ	soul, life	*psychiatrist, psychology*
ὥρα, ἡ	hour	*hour*

Appendix B: English-Greek Vocabulary Index

about	περί (with gen)
above	ὑπέρ (with acc.)
Abraham	Ἀβραάμ
again	πάλιν
against	κατά (with the genitive)
alone, only	μόνος
and, but	+δέ
and	καί
and I	κἀγώ
answer, I (takes dat)	ἀποκρίνομαι
apostle	ἀπόστολος, ὁ
bad	κακός
baptize, I	βαπτίζω
bear, I	φέρω
because, that	ὅτι
become, I	γίνομαι
before	πρό (with gen)
begin, I	ἄρχομαι
beginning	ἀρχή, ἡ
believe, I	πιστεύω
blind man	τυφλός, ὁ
boat	πλοῖον, τό
book	βιβλίον, τό
bread	ἄρτος, ὁ
brother	ἀδελφός, ὁ
but	ἀλλά
cast out, I	ἐκβάλλω
child	τέκνον, τό
church	ἐκκλησία, ἡ
come, I go	ἔρχομαι
commandment	ἐντολή, ἡ
country	χώρα, ἡ

cross	σταυρός, ὁ
crowd	ὄχλος, ὁ
cut	κόπτω
cry out, I	κράζω
day	ἡμέρα, ἡ
dead	νεκρός
death	θάνατος, ὁ
demon	δαιμόνιον, τό
desert	ἔρημος, ἡ
die, I	ἀποθνήσκω
disciple	μαθητής, ὁ
door	θύρα, ἡ
drink, I	πίνω
earth	γῆ, ἡ
eat, I	ἐσθίω
evil	πονηρός
eye	ὀφθαλμός, ὁ
face	πρόσωπον, τό
faithful	πιστός
fall, I	πίπτω
farmer	γεωργός, ὁ
field	ἀγρός, ὁ
find, I	εὑρίσκω
first	πρῶτος
forgive, I	χαρίζομαι
from	ἀπό (with the genitive)
from	παρά (with gen)
fruit	καρπός, ὁ
Galilee	Γαλιλαία, ἡ
gift	δῶρον, τό
glorify, I	δοξάζω
go, I	βαίνω

go down, I	καταβαίνω
go in, enter, I	εἰσέρχομαι
go out, I	ἐξέρχομαι
go through, I	διέρχομαι
go up, I	ἀναβαίνω
God	θεός, ὁ
good (beautiful)	καλός
good (moral)	ἀγαθός
gospel	εὐαγγέλιον, τό
have, I	ἔχω
heal, I	θεραπεύω
hear, I	ἀκούω
heart	καρδία, ἡ
heaven	οὐρανός, ὁ
hide, I	καλύπτω
holy	ἅγιος
honor	τιμή, ἡ
hour	ὥρα, ἡ
house	οἰκία , ἡ
house	οἶκος, ὁ
I	ἐγώ
if	εἰ
in	ἐν (with dative)
instead of	ἀντί (with genitive)
into	εἰς (with accusative)
Jesus	Ἰησοῦς
Jew	Ἰουδαῖος
joy	χαρά, ἡ
judge, I	κρίνω
kill, I	ἀποκτείνω
kingdom	βασιλεία, ἡ
know, I	γινώσκω

last	ἔσχατος
law	νόμος, ὁ
lead, I	ἄγω
life	βίος, ὁ
life	ζωή, ἡ
loose, I	λύω
lord	κύριος, ὁ
love	ἀγάπη, ἡ
man	ἄνθρωπος, ὁ
messenger, angel	ἄγγελος, ὁ
Messiah, Christ	Χριστός, ὁ
not	οὐ
not yet	οὔπω
now	νῦν
obey, I	ὑπακούω
open, I	ἀνοίγω
other	ἄλλος
out of	ἐκ/ἐξ (with the genitive)
owe, I	ὀφείλω
parable	παραβολή, ἡ
peace	εἰρήνη, ἡ
people	δῆμος, ὁ
persecute, I	διώκω
persuade, I	πείθω
Pharisee	Φαρισαῖος, ὁ
place	τόπος, ὁ
power	ἐξουσία, ἡ
praise, blessing	εὐλογία, ἡ
preach, I	εὐαγγελίζομαι
preach, I	κηρύσσω
presence, coming	παρουσία, ἡ
prison	φυλακή, ἡ

promise	ἐπαγγελία, ἡ
prophet	προφήτης, ὁ
raise up, I	ἐγείρω
rebuke, I	ἐλέγχω
receive, I	δέχομαι
receive, I	παραλαμβάνω
rejoice, am glad, I	χαίρω
remain, I	μένω
reveal, I	γνωρίζω
righteous	δίκαιος
righteousness	δικαιοσύνη, ἡ
road, way	ὁδός, ἡ
rock	πέτρα, ἡ
rule, I	ἄρχω
salvation	σωτηρία, ἡ
save, I	σῴζω
say, I	λέγω
second	δεύτερος
see, I	βλέπω
send, I	ἀποστέλλω
send, I	πέμπω
sheep	πρόβατον, τό
sign	σημεῖον, τό
sin	ἁμαρτία, ἡ
sin, I	ἁμαρτάνω
sing, I	ᾄδω
sinner	ἁμαρτωλός, ὁ
sister	ἀδελφή, ἡ
slave	δοῦλος, ὁ
small, little	μικρός
son	υἱός, ὁ
soul, life	ψυχή, ἡ

sow, I	σπείρω
stadium	στάδιον, τό
stone	λίθος, ὁ
suffer, I	πάσχω
sun	ἥλιος, ὁ
synagogue	συναγωγή, ἡ
take, I	λαμβάνω
take up, I take away	αἴρω
teach, I	διδάσκω
teacher	διδάσκαλος, ὁ
temple	ἱερόν, τό
ten	δέκα
testimony	μαρτυρία, ἡ
think	λογίζομαι
throne	θρόνος, ὁ
through	διά ΄ (with the genitive)
throw, I	βάλλω
time	χρόνος, ὁ
truth	ἀλήθεια, ἡ
under	ὑπό (with acc.)
verily, truly, amen	ἀμήν
village	κώμη, ἡ
voice	φωνή, ἡ
wedding	γάμος, ὁ
wisdom	σοφία, ἡ
wish, desire, I	βούλομαι
wish, I	θέλω
with	μετά (with the genitive)
with	σύν (with dative)
work	ἔργον, τό
work, I	ἐργάζομαι
world	κόσμος, ὁ

word	λόγος, ὁ
write, I	γράφω
writing, Scripture	γραφή, ἡ
you	σύ
young man	νεανίας, ὁ

Appendix C: Bible verses

῾Η ἀγάπη οὐδέποτε ἐκπίπτει.

Love never fails.

ΠΡΟΣ ΚΟΡΙΝΘΙΟΥΣ Α
I Corinthians 13:8

῾Ο λόγος ὁ σὸς ἀλήθειά ἐστι.

Your word is truth.

ΚΑΤΑ ΙΩΑΝΝΗΝ 17:17
John 17:17

Δόξα ἐν ὑψίστοις Θεῷ,

Καὶ ἐπὶ γῆς εἰρήνη,

᾿Εν ἀνθρώποις εὐδοκία!

Glory in the heights to God,
And on earth peace,
Among men good will!

ΚΑΤΑ ΛΟΥΚΑΝ 2:14
Luke 2:14

῾Η χάρις μετὰ πάντων ὑμῶν. ᾿Αμήν.

Grace be with all of you. Amen.

ΠΡΟΣ ΤΙΤΟΝ 3·15
Titus 3:15

Ἡμεῖς ἀγαπῶμεν αὐτὸν

ὅτι αὐτὸς πρῶτος ἠγάπησεν ἡμᾶς.

We love Him
because He first loved us.

ΙΩΑΝΝΟΥ Α 4:19
I John 4:19

Χαίρετε ἐν Κυρίῳ πάντοτε.

Πάλιν ἐρῶ, χαίρετε !

Rejoice in the Lord always.
Again I say, rejoice!

ΠΡΟΣ ΦΙΛΙΠΠΗΣΙΟΥΣ 4:4
To (the) Phillipians 4:4

Ἡ σωτηρία τῷ Θεῷ ἡμῶν

Τῷ καθημένῳ ἐπὶ τῷ θρόνῳ,

Καὶ τῷ Ἀρνίῳ

Salvation belongs to our God
To the One sitting on the throne,
And to the Lamb

ΑΠΟΚΑΛΥΨΙΣ 7·10
Revelation 7:10

Ἐγώ εἰμί ἡ ἄμπελος ἡ ἀληθινή,
καὶ ὁ Πατήρ μου ὁ γεωργός ἐστι.

I am the true vine,
And my Father is the farmer.

ΚΑΤΑ ΙΩΑΝΝΗΝ 15:1
(According to) John 15:1

Ἐγώ εἰμί ἡ ἄμπελος,
ὑμεῖς τὰ κλήματα.

I am the vine,
you are the branches.

ΚΑΤΑ ΙΩΑΝΝΗΝ 15:5
(According to) John 15:5

Appendix D: Reference charts

The Present Tense

–ω   –ομεν
–εις   –ετε
–ει   –ουσι

λύω	I loose	λύομεν	we loose
λύεις	you loose	λύετε	you loose
λύει	he looses	λύουσι	they loose

The Imperfect Tense

ἔλυον	I was loosing	ἐλύομεν	we were loosing
ἔλυες	you were loosing	ἐλύετε	you were loosing
ἔλυε	he was loosing	ἔλυον	they were loosing

Irregular Verb εἰμί

εἰμί	I am	ἐσμέν	we are
εἶ	you are	ἐστέ	you are
ἐστί	he is	εἰσί	they are

The Imperfect of εἰμί

ἤμην	I was	ἦμεν	we were
ἦς	you were	ἦτε	you were
ἦν	he was	ἦσαν	they were

The Deponent Verb

–ομαι	–ομεθα
–ῃ	–εσθε
–εται	–ονται

γίνομαι	I become	γινόμεθα	we become
γίνῃ	you become	γίνεσθε	you become
γίνεται	he becomes	γίνονται	they become

Second Declension Case Endings (Masculine)

singular		*plural*
–ος	N	–οι
–ου	G	–ων
–ῳ	D	–οις
–ον	A	–ους

Second Declension Case Endings (Neuter)

singular		*plural*
–ον	N	–α
–ου	G	–ων
–ῳ	D	–οις
–ον	A	–α

First Declension Case Endings (Feminine)

singular   *plural*

–α/η   N   –αι
–ας/ης   G   –ων
–ᾳ/ῃ   D   –αις
–αν/ην   A   –ας

First Declension Case Endings (Masculine)

singular   *plural*

–ας/ης   N   –αι
–ου/ου   G   –ων
–ᾳ/ῃ   D   –αις
–αν/ην   A   –ας

The Article "The"

ὁ   ἡ   τό   **N**   οἱ   αἱ   τά
τοῦ   τῆς   τοῦ   **G**   τῶν   τῶν   τῶν
τῷ   τῇ   τῷ   **D**   τοῖς   ταῖς   τοῖς
τόν   τήν   τό   **A**   τούς   τάς   τά

The Adjective

ἀγαθός   ἀγαθή   ἀγαθόν   N   ἀγαθοί   ἀγαθαί   ἀγαθά
ἀγαθόυ   ἀγαθῆς   ἀγαθοῦ   G   ἀγαθῶν   ἀγαθῶν   ἀγαθῶν
ἀγαθῶ   ἀγαθή   ἀγαθῷ   D   ἀγαθοῖς   ἀγαθαῖς   ἀγαθοῖς
ἀγαθὸν   ἀγαθήν   ἀγαθόν   A   ἀγαθούς   ἀγαθάς   ἀγαθά

First Person Personal Pronoun

ἐγώ	I	**N**	ἡμεῖς	we
μου	of me (my)	**G**	ἡμῶν	of us (our)
μοι	to me	**D**	ἡμῖν	to us
με	me	**A**	ἡμᾶς	us

Second Person Personal Pronoun

σύ	you	**N**	ὑμεῖς	you
σοῦ	of you (your)	**G**	ὑμων	of you (your)
σοί	to you	**D**	ὑμῖν	to you
σέ	you	**A**	ὑμᾶς	you

Appendix E: Grammar Review

In many ways, Greek is similar to English. The purpose of this review is to draw attention to these similarities, and also to further explain the areas where Greek and English grammar differ.

To begin with, Greek and English have the same parts of speech.

A **noun** is a naming word. It names a person, place, thing, or idea. Some examples of nouns are: *boat, faith, grass, nose, man, village.* A noun can have several different jobs in a sentence. In this course, we will study nouns as subjects, direct objects, indirect objects, and objects of prepositions.

A **pronoun** is a word that replaces a noun. *He, she, we,* and *they* are some pronouns. These words can be substituted for nouns in various parts of the sentence. The Greek pronoun-endings (part of all Greek verbs) are explained and used, as well as first and second person personal pronouns.

An **adjective** describes a noun. It answers the questions "Which one," "How many," or "What kind?" *Small, ten, many, red,* and *pretty* are all adjectives.

An **article** is really an adjective, but it is so common that it has the name *article* to distinguish it from the rest of the adjectives. There are three articles in English (*a, an, the*), but in Greek there is only one (*the*).

A **verb** is a word that shows action or being. The words *run, think, read, slither,* and *believe* are all actions. The being verbs are *am, is, are, was, were, be, being,* and *been.* In this course, we will learn verbs in the present and imperfect tenses, as well as a special group of present tense verbs called *deponents.*

A **preposition** is a word that joins a noun (called the object of the preposition) to a sentence. A preposition expresses relationship. *Under, about, through,* and *with* are prepositions. *A man goes under a bridge. The girl thinks about the book.*

These are the basic parts of speech which are introduced in this course. The higher your comfort level with English grammar, the easier it will be for you to understand Greek grammar.

In English, our understanding is based largely on the position a word has in the sentence. *The boy loves the dog* and *The dog loves the boy* express two completely different thoughts. In the first sentence, *boy* is the subject. It comes before the verb, and it answers the question "Who loves?" When the position of the words changed, the answer to the question "Who loves?" also changed. In the second sentence, *dog* is the subject. If I say, *The young boy loves the dog,* I know that the boy is young because the word *young* precedes the word *boy*. Notice how the meaning changes when we move the word *young*: *The boy loves the young dog.*

While the Greek language is fully capable of expressing these same ideas, it does not use word position to do so. Greek, like Latin, is an **inflected** language. This means that the language has a system of word endings which are used to show the part a word plays in a sentence. Word order is not as important in Greek. The *endings* are the clues to syntax. A student of Greek is in some ways like a detective, becoming aware of these clues and finding them in the sentence.

Greek nouns have five cases. The cases show the different functions of nouns in a sentence. Below, the cases are listed with their principal functions.

Nominative	Subject/ Predicate nominative
Genitive	Possessive (key word *of*)
Dative	Indirect object (key words *to/for*)
Accusative	Direct object
(Vocative	Direct address)[1]

My students regularly chant through a simplified version of this chart to help them remember the noun functions and their cases. The simplified version looks like this:

Nominative------Subject
Genitive----------*of a*
Dative------------*to/for*
Accusative-------D.O.

Each of the cases listed above has its own singular ending and its own plural ending. Listing a noun with all of its endings is called **declining** the noun. In this course, complete declensions are learned, and the four cases are used in translation and grammar work.

---

1 The vocative case is not covered in this course. In the sentence, *Mary, please close the door* the word *Mary* would be in the vocative case, because it indicates the person to whom the sentence is directed. Because the vocative has the same ending as the nominative in most declensions and genders, it is unnecessary to learn it as a separate ending.

Greek has three declensions. (The first two declensions are covered this year.) Each of the declensions has its own set of endings. There are some similarities between the endings, and these are noted in the text to aid in memorization. The declensions as they are taught in this course are listed in appendix D.

Greek verbs have their own endings as well. The verb endings differ from the noun endings, and they show the person and number to which the verb refers. An easy way to understand this is to think of the verb ending as equivalent to an English pronoun. The English phrase *We think* is shown by a single word in Greek which is made of two parts—the **stem**, which expresses the idea *think,* + the **ending**, which indicates the personal pronoun *we*. The ending changes when the pronoun changes. Writing a verb with all of its endings is called **conjugating** the verb. In this course, the present and the imperfect tenses are learned. The imperfect tense shows a continuing action in the past. It is shown in English by the use of the helping verbs *was* and *were*. *He was sitting* and *They were running* are examples of this type of continuing action. These conjugations are also listed in appendix B.

This is Greek grammar in its most simplistic terms. Now, let's look at a few examples of how this works. In these examples, diagrams and word classification are used to give a better picture of the different functions. These are important tools and should be used throughout the course to aid the student in the translation exercises.

Example 1:

> *A man eats.*

First, we identify the subject, verb, and any other words in the sentence. Asking "Who or what is the sentence about?" shows that *man* is the subject. The subject is written on the first horizontal line in a diagram. Next, we ask, "What does the man do?" The answer is, "He eats," so *eats* is the verb in this sentence. The verb is located next to the subject on the diagram, after a vertical line. The only other word left in this sentence is *a*, which is an article, and is located below *man* in the diagram because it modifies the word *man*.

> *article subject verb*
> A   man   eats.

Now, we can look at this sentence again, and determine which Greek word we will use for each of these words. I will begin with the word *man*, the subject of this sentence. Above, we listed subject as the function of the nominative case, so I know that *man* will have the nominative ending. The ending will also be singular, because we are talking about one man, not many men. In this case, the ending will be –ος. The nominative case tells us that this word is the subject of the sentence, so I can put this word first, last, or in the middle of the sentence. No matter where it is, it will always be the subject.

Remember that in Greek there is no word for *a*. This word is not translated.

The word *eats* is the verb. Because we need to include the pronoun ending in Greek, we can think of it as *he eats*. The present indicative ending for *he* (3rd person singular) is –ει.

ἄνθρωπος ἐσθίει.
ἐσθίει ἄνθρωπος.

These sentences both say the same thing.

Example 2:

> *The first son of a teacher believes.*

Here again, we begin by asking our standard questions to determine who the sentence is about and what he is doing (subject and verb). Next, we see that the words *the* and *first* modify our subject by answering the question, "Which son?" On the diagram, they are located on slanted lines below the subject. Notice also that one of our key words is in this sentence. The word *of* should immediately make us think of the genitive case. The whole phrase *of a teacher* is translated by the single word *teacher* with the genitive (*of a*) ending.

article	adjective	subject	possessive	verb
The	first	son	of a teacher	believes.

The subject will be in the nominative case. Any articles or adjectives take the same case as the word they modify. That means that *the* and *first* are in the nominative case as well. We have already noted that the phrase *of a teacher* is in the genitive case. *Believes*, or *he believes*, takes the 3rd person singular ending.

ὁ πρῶτος υἱὸς διδασκάλου πιστεύει.
The first   son   of a teacher   (he)believes.

Here the sentence order looks very much like a typical English sentence. But remember, we can change the sentence order around and still say the same thing.

πιστεύει ὁ πρῶτος υἱὸς διδασκάλου.

πιστεύει διδασκάλου ὁ πρῶτος υἱὸς.

Example 3:

The only servant in the house was sending a gift .

By asking "Who or what is this sentence about?" and "What is he doing?", we determine that *servant* is the subject of the sentence and *was sending* is the verb. Be careful to include helping verbs in your diagram. Without the word *was*, you would be likely to miss that this verb must be translated into the imperfect tense in Greek. Next, we can see that *the* and *only* will go under *servant* on the diagram because they tell us **which** servant. *In the house*, as a prepositional phrase answering **which**, will also go under *servant*. At this point, you may find it helpful to put a small *d* on your diagram above the word *house* to serve as a reminder that this word must be in the dative case when you translate it. Next, we can ask **what** the servant was sending. The answer, *gift*, will go next to the verb as the direct object.

article	adjective	subject	preposition	article	object-of-prep	verb	article	direct object
The	only	servant	in	the	house	was sending	a	gift.

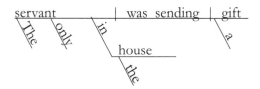

The subject, once again, is in the nominative case, as are its modifiers (*the* and *only*). The phrase *in the house* is a prepositional phrase, and by remembering that ἐν takes the dative, we know that the word *house* is in the dative case (οἴκῳ). From there, we look at the verb, *was sending*. The helping verb *was* indicates that this will be in the imperfect tense in Greek (ἔπεμπε). Finally, the word *gift* is the direct object, so it will be in the accusative case (δῶρον).

ὁ μόνος δοῦλος ἐν τῷ οἴκῳ ἔπεμπε δῶρον.
The only servant in the house was sending gift.

Remember, changing the word order does not change the meaning of the sentence.

ἔπεμπε δῶρον ὁ δοῦλος ἐν τῷ οἴκῳ ὁ μόνος.

δῶρον ὁ δοῦλος ὁ μόνος ἐν τῷ οἴκῳ ἔπεμπε.

Appendix F: Workbook Answer Key

Lesson 1.2

Γ gamma	Δ delta	Η eta
Λ lambda	Ξ theta	Σ sigma
Υ upsilon	Ω omega	

Lesson 1.3

Ω ω	Τ τ	Η η
Σ σ, ς	Α α	Ρ ρ
Υ υ	Γ γ	Ψ ψ
Β β	Λ λ	Φ φ
Χ χ	Δ δ	Ξ ξ
Ε ε	Ο ο	Μ μ
Ι ι	Ζ ζ	Θ θ
Κ κ	Ν ν	Π π

Lesson 1.4

κατα ματθαιον
προς ρωμαιους
προς γαλατας
προς φιλημονα
ιωαννου α

Lesson 1.5

Which form of sigma is used at the end of a word? __ς
Two gammas together make the __/ng/__ sound.

Lesson 2.1

ἀκούω	I hear
βλέπω	I see
ἔχω	I have or hold
λύω	I loose or destroy
πιστεύω	I believe

γινώσκω	I know
γράφω	I write
λαμβάνω	I take
λέγω	I say or speak
πάσχω	I suffer
βάλλω	I throw
διδάσκω	I teach
ἐγείρω	I raise up
ἄγω	I lead
μένω	I remain
πέμπω	I send
φέρω	I bear, bring
βαπτίζω	I baptize
κρίνω	I judge
σώζω	I save
βαίνω	I go
ἁμαρτάνω	I sin
ἀποστέλλω	I send
θέλω	I wish
καλύπτω	I hide

Lesson 2.2

-ω	I		-ομεν	we
-εις	you (s)		-ετε	you
-ει	he, she, it		-ουσι	they

γράφω	I write	γράφομεν	we write
γράφεις	you write	γράφετε	you write
γράφει	he writes	γράφουσι	they write

γινώσκω	γινώσκομεν	λαμβάνω	λαμβάνομε
γινώσκεις	γινώσκετε	λαμβάνεις	λαμβάνετε
γινώσκει	γινώσκουσι	λαμβάνει	λαμβάνουσ

λέγω	λέγομεν	πάσχω	πάσχομεν
λέγεις	λέγετε	πάσχεις	πάσχετε
λέγει	λέγουσι	πάσχει	πάσχουσι

Lesson 2.3

εἰμί	I am	ἐσμέν	we are
εἶ	you (s) are	ἐστέ	you (p) are
ἐστί	he is	εἰσί	they are

ἄγω	ἄγομεν	μένω	μένομεν
ἄγεις	ἄγετε	μένεις	μένετε
ἄγει	ἄγουσι	μένει	μένουσι

πέμπω	πέμπομεν	φέρω	φέρομεν
πέμπεις	πέμπετε	φέρεις	φέρετε
πέμπει	πέμπουσι	φέρει	φέρουσι

Lesson 2.4

λαμβάνετε	you (p) take
σώζουσι	they save
κρίνομεν	we judge
πέμπει	he, she, it sends
διδάσκομεν	we teach
ἀκούετε	you (p) hear
πιστεύετε	you (p) believe
βαπτίζεις	you (s) baptize
ἐγείρουσι	they raise up
μένω	I remain

Lesson 2.5

καλύπτω	I hide
ἁμαρτάνω	I sin
σώζω	I save
λύω	I loose / destroy
μένω	I remain
κρίνω	I judge
πάσχω	I suffer
ἄγω	I lead
γινώσκω	I know
πιστεύω	I believe
θέλω	I wish
λαμβάνω	I take
βλέπω	I see
ἐγείρω	I raise up
γράφω	I write
βαπτίζω	I baptize
βάλλω	I throw
φέρω	I bear / bring
πέμπω	I send
διδάσκω	I teach
βαίνω	I go
ἀποστέλλω	I send
ἔχω	I have / hold
λέγω	I say / speak
ἀκούω	I hear

Lesson 3.1

ὁ ἄγγελος	the messenger, angel
ὁ λόγος	the word
ὁ νόμος	the law

ὁ βίος	the life
ὁ θεός	the God
ὁ ἀγρός	the field
ὁ ἀπόστολος	the apostle
ὁ ἀδελφός	the brother
ὁ ἄνθρωπος	the man
ὁ δοῦλος	the slave
ὁ κόσμος	the world
ὁ θάνατος	the death
ὁ οἶκος	the house
ὁ υἱός	the son
ὁ κύριος	the lord
ὁ λίθος	the stone
ὁ οὐρανός	the heaven
ὁ τόπος	the place
ὁ διδάσκαλος	the teacher
ὁ ἁμαρτωλός	the sinner
ὁ ἄρτος	the bread
ὁ τυφλός	the blind man
ὁ Ἰουδαῖος	the Jew
ὁ καρπός	the fruit
ὁ Φαρισαῖος	the Pharisee
ὁ Χριστός	the Christ

Lesson 3.2

ἄνθρωπος	ἄνθρωποι
ἀνθρώπου	ἀνθρώπων
ἀνθρώπῳ	ἀνθρώποις
ἄνθρωπον	ἀνθρώπους

θεός	θεοί
θεοῦ	θεῶν
θεῷ	θεοῖς
θεόν	θεούς

οὐρανός	οὐρανοί
οὐρανοῦ	οὐρανῶν
οὐρανῷ	οὐρανοῖς
οὐρανόν	οὐρανούς

ἁμαρτωλός	ἁμαρτωλοί
ἁμαρτωλοῦ	ἁμαρτωλῶν
ἁμαρτωλῷ	ἁμαρτωλοῖς
ἁμαρτωλόν	ἁμαρτωλούς

Lesson 3.3

τό τέκνον	the child
τό εὐαγγέλιον	the gospel
τό πρόσωπον	the face
τό ἱερόν	the temple
τό δῶρον	the gift
τό βιβλίον	the book
τό δαιμόνιον	the demon
τό ἔργον	the work
τό πλοῖον	the boat

1. πρόσωπον
2. πλοῖον
3. βιβλίον
4. δῶρον
5. δαιμόνιον
6. ἱερόν

Lesson 3.4

ἄνθρωπος	ἄνθρωποι
ἀνθρώπου	ἀνθρώπων
ἀνθρώπῳ	ἀνθρώποις
ἄνθρωπον	ἀνθρώπους

δῶρον	δῶρα
δώρου	δώρων
δώρῳ	δώροις
δῶρον	δῶρα

ἀλήθεια	ἀλήθειαι
ἀληθείας	ἀληθειῶν
ἀληθείᾳ	ἀληθείαις
ἀλήθειαν	ἀληθείας

βιβλίον	βιβλίοι
βιβλίου	βιβλίων
βιβλίῳ	βιβλίοις
βιβλίον	βιβλίους

Lesson 3.5

Lesson 4.1

ἡ ἀλήθεια	the truth
ἡ καρδία	the heart
ἡ ζωή	the life
ἡ ἐπαγγελία	the promise
ἡ εἰρήνη	the peace

ἡ ὥρα	the hour
ἡ παραβολή	the parable
ἡ χαρά	the joy
ἡ ἐκκλησία	the church
ἡ ἁμαρτία	the sin

ἡ βασιλεία	the kingdom
ἡ ψυχή	the soul/life
ἡ ἡμέρα	the day
ἡ ἐντολή	the commandment
ἡ οἰκία	the house

ἡ φωνή	the voice
ἡ ἀγάπη	the love
ἡ γραφή	the writing/scripture

Lesson 4.2

ἐκκλησία	ἐκκλησίαι
ἐκκλησίας	ἐκκλησιῶν
ἐκκλησίᾳ	ἐκκλησίαις
ἐκκλησίαν	ἐκκλησίας

χαρά	χαραί
χαρᾶς	χαρῶν
χαρᾷ	χαραῖς
χαράν	χαράς

παραβολή	παραβολαί
παραβολῆς	παραβολῶν
παραβολῇ	παραβολαῖς
παραβολήν	παραβολάς

καρδία	καρδίαι
καρδίας	καρδιῶν
καρδίᾳ	καρδίαις
καρδίαν	καρδίας

πάσχω	I suffer	πάσχομεν	we suffer
πάσχεις	you suffer	πάσχετε	you suffer
πάσχει	he suffers	πάσχουσι	they suffer

φέρω	I bring	φέρομεν	we bring
φέρεις	you bring	φέρετε	you bring
φέρει	he brings	φέρουσι	they bring

εἰμί	I am	ἐσμέν	we are
εἶ	you (s) are	ἐστέ	you are
ἐστί	he is	εἰσί	they are

Lesson 4.3

	Gender	Number	Case	translation
θεοῦ	M	S	G	God
ἀλήθεια	F	S	N	truth
ζωήν	F	S	A	life
ἀνθρώπους	M	P	A	men
πλοῖον	N	S	N/A	boat
λίθου	M	S	G	stone
τέκνων	N	P	G	children
χαραῖς	F	P	D	joys

Lesson 4.4

ἄνθρωπός	ἐστι	δοῦλος.
A man	is	a slave.

δοῦλοι	θεοῦ	πιστεύουσι.
Slaves	of God	believe.

τέκνα	ἀκούουσι.
Children	hear.

χαρά	ἀγγέλων	μένει.
Joy	of angels	remains.

τυφλὸς	πάσχει.
A blind man	suffers.

Lesson 4.5

τέκνον	τέκνα
τέκνου	τέκνων
τέκνῳ	τέκνοις
τέκνον	τέκνα

οἰκία	οἰκίαι
οἰκίας	οἰκιῶν
οἰκίᾳ	οἰκίαις
οἰκίαν	οἰκίας

εἰμί	ἐσμέν	λέγω	λέγομεν
εἶ	ἐστέ	λέγεις	λέγετε
ἐστί	εἰσί	λέγει	λέγουσι

Lesson 5.1

κακός	bad
δίκαιος	righteous
ἀγαθός	good (moral)
ἅγιος	holy
ἔσχατος	last

παρά	from
κατά	against
διά	through
πρό	before
μετά	with

ἄλλος	other
πιστός	faithful
δεύτερος	second
καλός	good, beautiful
πρῶτος	first

περί	about
ἀπό	from
ἐκ / ἐξ	out of

Lesson 5.2

Singular

Nom.	κακός	κακή	κακόν
Gen.	κακοῦ	κακῆς	κακοῦ
Dat.	κακῷ	κακῇ	κακῷ
Acc.	κακόν	κακήν	κακόν

Plural

Nom.	κακοί	κακαί	κακά
Gen.	κακῶν	κακῶν	κακῶν
Dat.	κακοῖς	κακαῖς	κακοῖς
Acc.	κακούς	κακάς	κακά

Singular

Nom.	πιστός	πιστή	πιστόν
Gen.	πιστοῦ	πιστῆς	πιστοῦ
Dat.	πιστῷ	πιστῇ	πιστῷ
Acc.	πιστόν	πιστήν	πιστόν

Plural

Nom.	πιστοί	πισταί	πιστά
Gen.	πιστῶν	πιστῶν	πιστῶν
Dat.	πιστοῖς	πισταῖς	πιστοῖς
Acc.	πιστούς	πιστάς	πιστά

Singular

Nom.	καλός	καλή	καλόν
Gen.	καλοῦ	καλῆς	καλοῦ
Dat.	καλῷ	καλῇ	καλῷ
Acc.	καλόν	καλήν	καλόν

Plural

Nom.	καλοί	καλαί	καλά
Gen.	καλῶν	καλῶν	καλῶν
Dat.	καλοῖς	καλαῖς	καλοῖς
Acc.	καλούς	καλάς	καλά

Lesson 5.3

Answers will vary.

Lesson 5.4

against God	κατὰ θεοῦ
with men	μετὰ ἀνθρώπων
out of churches	ἐξ ἐκκλησιῶν
through a book	διὰ βιβλίου
about children	περὶ τέκνων

Singular

Nom.	πρῶτος	πρώτη	πρῶτον
Gen.	πρώτου	πρώτης	πρώτου
Dat.	πρώτῳ	πρώτῃ	πρώτῳ
Acc.	πρῶτον	πρώτην	πρῶτον

Plural

Nom.	πρῶτοι	πρῶται	πρῶτα
Gen.	πρώτων	πρώτων	πρώτων
Dat.	πρώτοις	πρώταις	πρώτοις
Acc.	πρώτους	πρώτας	πρῶτα

Singular

Nom.	ἅγιος	ἁγία	ἅγιον
Gen.	ἁγίου	ἁγίας	ἁγίου
Dat.	ἁγίῳ	ἁγίᾳ	ἁγίῳ
Acc.	ἅγιον	ἁγίαν	ἅγιον

Plural

Nom.	ἅγιοι	ἅγιαι	ἅγια
Gen.	ἁγίων	ἁγίων	ἁγίων
Dat.	ἁγίοις	ἁγίαις	ἁγίοις
Acc.	ἁγίους	ἁγίας	ἅγια

Lesson 5.5

Textbook:

Where does the good son go?
The good son goes through the field.
With whom does he go?
He goes with the apostle.
What does the apostle teach the son?
He teaches the son about God.
Who are faithful men?
The apostle and the son are faithful men.

Workbook:

	Gender	Number	Case	translation
τοῦ ἀγροῦ	M	S	G	of the field
ἀληθείας	F	S	G	of truth
διδάσκαλος	M	S	N	a teacher
θεοῦ	M	S	G	God
πιστοὶ ἄνθρωποι	M	P	N	faithful men

εἰμί	ἐσμέν	ἀκούω	ἀκούομεν
εἶ	ἐστέ	ἀκούεις	ἀκούετε
ἐστί	εἰσί	ἀκούει	ἀκούουσι

<table>
<tr><td>Lesson 6.1</td><td></td><td></td></tr>
</table>

ἄνθρωπος	Nominative	ἄνθρωποι
ἀνθρώπου	Genitive	ἀνθρώπων
ἀνθρώπῳ	Dative	ἀνθρώποις
ἄνθρωπον	Accusative	ἀνθρώπους

δῶρον	Nominative	δῶρα
δώρου	Genitive	δώρων
δώρῳ	Dative	δώροις
δῶρον	Accusative	δῶρα

Lesson 6.2

	Gender	Number	Case	translation
λόγῳ	M	S	D	to/for a word
θεόν	M	S	A	God
προσώποις	N	P	D	to/for faces
κύριῳ	M	S	D	to/for a lord
πλοῖα	N	P	A	boats
τέκνον	N	S	A	child
οἴκους	M	P	A	houses
βιβλίοις	N	P	D	to/for books
διδασκάλῳ	M	S	D	to/for a teacher
εὐαγγέλια	N	P	A	churches

Lesson 6.3

ἀλήθεια	Nominative	ἀλήθειαι
ἀληθείας	Genitive	ἀλήθειῶν
ἀληθείᾳ	Dative	ἀληθείαις
ἀλήθειαν	Accusative	ἀληθείας

γραφή	Nominative	γραφαί
γραφῆς	Genitive	γραφῶν
γραφῇ	Dative	γραφαῖς
γραφήν	Accusative	γραφάς

	Gender	Number	Case	translation
ὥραν	F	S	A	hour
φωνάς	F	P	A	voices
βασιλείᾳ	F	S	D	to/for a kingdom
ἐκκλησίαις	F	P	D	to/for churches
καρδίας	F	P	A	hearts

Lesson 6.4

	Gender	Number	Case	translation
πλοῖα	N	P	N/A	boats
βασιλείαν	F	S	A	kingdom
εἰρήνη	F	S	G	of peace
ἄρτων	M	P	G	of breads

ἱεροῦ	N	S	G	of a temple
εὐαγγελίοις	N	P	D	to/for gospels
ἁμαρτωλόν	M	S	A	sinner
ἁμαρτίᾳ	F	S	D	to/for sin
ἡμέραις	F	P	D	to /for days
κόσμῳ	M	S	D	to/for a world

	Singular		
Nom.	ἀγαθός	ἀγαθή	ἀγαθόν
Gen.	ἀγαθοῦ	ἀγαθῆς	ἀγαθοῦ
Dat.	ἀγαθῷ	ἀγαθῇ	ἀγαθῷ
Acc.	ἀγαθόν	ἀγαθήν	ἀγαθόν
	Plural		
Nom.	ἀγαθοί	ἀγαθαί	ἀγαθά
Gen.	ἀγαθῶν	ἀγαθῶν	ἀγαθῶν
Dat.	ἀγαθοῖς	ἀγαθαῖς	ἀγαθοῖς
Acc.	ἀγαθούς	ἀγαθάς	ἀγαθά

Lesson 6.5

εἰμί	ἐσμέν	ἐγείρω	ἐγείρομεν
εἶ	ἐστέ	ἐγείρεις	ἐγείρετε
ἐστί	εἰσί	ἐγείρει	ἐγείρουσι

Lesson 7.1

ὁ ἄγγελος	angel/messenger
βάλλω	I throw
δέκα	ten
ὁ λόγος	the word
διδάσκω	I teach

Lesson 7.2

	Singular		
Nom.	ἅγιος	ἁγία	ἅγιον
Gen.	ἁγίου	ἁγίας	ἁγίου
Dat.	ἁγίῳ	ἁγίᾳ	ἁγίῳ
Acc.	ἅγιον	ἁγίαν	ἅγιον
	Plural		
Nom.	ἅγιοι	ἅγιαι	ἅγια
Gen.	ἁγίων	ἁγίων	ἁγίων
Dat.	ἁγίοις	ἁγίαις	ἁγίοις
Acc.	ἁγίους	ἁγίας	ἅγια

	Singular		
Nom.	κακός	κακή	κακόν
Gen.	κακοῦ	κακῆς	κακοῦ
Dat.	κακῷ	κακῇ	κακῷ
Acc.	κακόν	κακήν	κακόν
	Plural		
Nom.	κακοί	κακαί	κακά
Gen.	κακῶν	κακῶν	κακῶν
Dat.	κακοῖς	κακαῖς	κακοῖς
Acc.	κακούς	κακάς	κακά

ἐκβάλλω	I cast out	ἐκβάλλομεν	we cast out
ἐκβάλλεις	you cast out	ἐκβάλλετε	you cast out
ἐκβάλλει	he casts out	ἐκβάλλουσι	they cast out

Sally and her father dry ~~the dishes~~.
The little boy ~~kicked the ball~~ across the field.
I'm ~~going to read~~ ~~this book~~ before bed.
The teacher ~~instructs~~ the wayward ~~children~~.

Lesson 7.3

ἄνθρωπος	ἄνθρωποι
ἀνθρώπου	ἀνθρώπων
ἀνθρώπῳ	ἀνθρώποις
ἄνθρωπον	ἀνθρώπους

δῶρον	δῶρα
δώρου	δώρων
δώρῳ	δώροις
δῶρον	δῶρα

ἀλήθεια	ἀλήθειαι
ἀληθείας	ἀληθειῶν
ἀληθείᾳ	ἀληθείαις
ἀλήθειαν	ἀληθείας

Acc. endings	Singular	Plural
2nd declension M	–ον	–ους
2nd declension N	–ον	–α
1st declension F	–α / –η	–ας

angel   ἄγγελον
book   βιβλίον
children   τέκνα
temples   ἱερά
fields   ἀγρούς

Lesson 7.4

εἰμί	I am		ἐσμέν	we are
εἶ	you (s) are		ἐστέ	you are
ἐστί	he is		εἰσί	they are

    S   V   DO
A son eats bread.
υἱός ἐσθίει ἄρτον.

    S   V   DO
Apostles baptize sinners.
ἀπόστολοι βαπτίζουσι ἁμαρτωλούς.

    S   V   DO
God judges a heart.
ὁ θεός κρίνει καρδίαν.[1]

    S   V   DO
A man sees a kingdom.
ἄνθρωπος βλέπει βασιλείαν.

    S   V   DO
A child throws a book.
τέκνον βάλλει βιβλίον.

Lesson 8.1

ὁ νόμος   the name
ὁ θεός   the god
ὁ ἀπόστολος   the apostle
ὁ βίος   the life
ὁ ἀγρός   the field

Lesson 8.2

Textbook:
Nominative: *used as subject or predicate nominative*
Gen: *shows possession (of…), & used with some prep.s*
Acc.: *used as direct object, and as object of some prepositions*

---

[1] When the name of God is written in Greek, it usually includes the article. The word *god* without the article can refer to one of many gods, as opposed to the true God. A translation that doesn't include the article should not be counted wrong, but it should nonetheless be pointed out to the student why the article is often included.

Workbook:

θέλω	θέλομεν	ἁμαρτάνω	ἁμαρτάνομεν
θέλεις	θέλετε	ἁμαρτάνεις	ἁμαρτάνετε
θέλει	θέλουσι	ἁμαρτάνει	ἁμαρτάνουσι

	Gender	Number	Case	translation
ἁμαρτωλοί	M	P	N	sinners
σταυρούς	M	P	A	crosses
χώρας	F	S	G	of a country
(also)	F	P	A	countries
σταυρόν	M	S	A	cross
ἀποστόλου	M	S	G	of an apostle

Lesson 8.3

ἄνθρωπος	ἄνθρωποι
ἀνθρώπου	ἀνθρώπων
ἀνθρώπῳ	ἀνθρώποις
ἄνθρωπον	ἀνθρώπους

δῶρον	δῶρα
δώρου	δώρων
δώρῳ	δώροις
δῶρον	δῶρα

ἀλήθεια	ἀλήθειαι
ἀληθείας	ἀληθειῶν
ἀληθείᾳ	ἀληθείαις
ἀλήθειαν	ἀληθείας

S V
A crowd hears.
ὄχλος ἀκούει.

S V DO
A crowd hears words.
ὄχλος ἀκούει λόγους.

adj S V DO poss
A faithful crowd hears words of God.
πιστὸς ὄχλος ἀκούει λόγους τοῦ θεοῦ.

S _V_ DO
An apostle casts out a demon.
ἀπόστολος ἐκβάλλει δαιμόνιον.

S V DO
A child sees a country.
τέκνον βλέπει χώραν.

Lesson 8.4

εἰμί	I am		ἐσμέν	we are
εἶ	you (s) are		ἐστέ	you are
ἐστί	he is		εἰσί	they are

adj S V DO
ὁ ἅγιος θεὸς ἀκούει δούλους.
The holy God hears slaves.

adj S V adj DO
ὁ ἅγιος θεὸς ἀκούει πιστοὺς δούλους.
The holy God hears faithful slaves.

S V prep OP
ὁ διδάσκαλος διδάσκει περὶ ἀληθείας.
The teacher teaches about truth.

S poss V prep
ὁ διδάσκαλος τοῦ εὐαγγελίου διδάσκει περὶ
OP poss
ἀληθείας τοῦ λόγου.
The teacher of the gospel teaches about the word's
truth. (the truth of the word)

S poss V
οἱ διδάσκαλοι τοῦ εὐαγγελίου διδάσκουσι
DO poss
τὸν λόγον τοῦ θεοῦ.
The teachers of the gospel teach the word of God.

Lesson 8.5

Lesson 9.1

ὁ ἀδελφός	the brother
ὁ δοῦλος	the slave
ὁ ἄνθρωπος	the man
ὁ κόσμος	the world
καί	and

Lesson 9.2

πίπτω	πίπτομεν	σώζω	σώζομεν
πίπτεις	πίπτετε	σώζεις	σώζετε
πίπτει	πίπτουσι	σώζει	σώζουσι

	Gender	Number	Case	translation
ἄρτοις	M	P	D	to/for breads
ἁμαρτωλόν	M	S	A	sinner
ἀγάπη	F	S	D	to/for love
ἀγγέλους	M	P	A	angels
τέκνα	N	P	N/A	children
λίθῳ	M	S	D	to/for a stone
ζωαῖς	F	P	D	to /for lives
φωνήν	F	S	G	of a voice
δῶρον	N	S	N/A	gift
θανάτους	M	P	A	deaths

Lesson 9.3

ἄνθρωπος	ἄνθρωποι
ἀνθρώπου	ἀνθρώπων
ἀνθρώπῳ	ἀνθρώποις
ἄνθρωπον	ἀνθρώπους

δῶρον	δῶρα
δώρου	δώρων
δώρῳ	δώροις
δῶρον	δῶρα

ἀλήθεια	ἀλήθειαι
ἀληθείας	ἀληθειῶν
ἀληθείᾳ	ἀληθείαις
ἀλήθειαν	ἀληθείας

into a temple	εἰς ἱερόν
in churches	ἐν ἐκκλησίαις
with God	σὺν θεῷ or σὺν τῷ θεῷ
under a stone	ὑπὸ λίθον
above angels	ὑπὲρ ἀγγέλους

Lesson 9.4

εἰμί	ἐσμέν	διδάσκω	διδάσκομεν
εἶ	ἐστέ	διδάσκεις	διδάσκετε
ἐστί	εἰσί	διδάσκει	διδάσκουσι

S   V prep OP
A servant goes into a temple.
δοῦλος βαίνει εἰς ἱερόν.

S   V prep OP
An apostle teaches in churches.
ἀπόστολος διδάσκει ἐν ἐκκλησίαις.

S   V prep OP
A child is with a man.
τέκνον ἐστὶ σὺν ἄνθρωπος.

S   V prep OP
It remains under a stone.
μένει ὑπὸ λίθον.

S   V prep OP
God is above angels.
ὁ θεός ἐστιν ὑπὲρ ἀγγέλους.

Lesson 9.5

	Singular		
Nom.	ἔσχατος	ἐσχάτη	ἔσχατον
Gen.	ἐσχάτου	ἐσχάτης	ἐσχάτου
Dat.	ἐσχάτῳ	ἐσχάτη	ἐσχάτῳ
Acc.	ἔσχατον	ἐσχάτην	ἔσχατον
	Plural		
Nom.	ἔσχατοι	ἔσχαται	ἔσχατα
Gen.	ἐσχάτων	ἐσχάτων	ἐσχάτων
Dat.	ἐσχάτοις	ἐσχάταις	ἐσχάτοις
Acc.	ἐσχάτους	ἐσχάτας	ἔσχατα

	Singular		
Nom.	πιστός	πιστή	πιστόν
Gen.	πιστοῦ	πιστῆς	πιστοῦ
Dat.	πιστῷ	πιστῆ	πιστῷ
Acc.	πιστόν	πιστήν	πιστόν
	Plural		
Nom.	πιστοί	πισταί	πιστά
Gen.	πιστῶν	πιστῶν	πιστῶν
Dat.	πιστοῖς	πισταῖς	πιστοῖς
Acc.	πιστούς	πιστάς	πιστά

Lesson 10.1

ἡ ἀρχή	the beginning
ἡ χώρα	the country
πίπτω	I fall
ἡ θύρα	the door
ὁ σταυρός	the cross
ἐν (w/ dat)	in
εἰς (w/ acc)	into
παρά (w/ gen)	from
ἐκβάλλω	i cast out
ὁ ὄχλος	the crowd

ἡ ἀδελφή	the sister
ἡ πέτρα	the rock
ἡ τιμή	the honor
σύν *(w/ dat)*	with
ὑπό *(w/ acc)*	under
ὑπέρ *(w/ acc)*	above

Lesson 10.2

πάσχω	I suffer	πάσχομεν	we suffer
πάσχεις	you suffer	πάσχετε	you suffer
πάσχει	he suffers	πάσχουσι	they suffer

σὺν ἀδελφή	with a sister
ὑπὸ πέτρας	under rocks
εἰς χώραν	into a country
ὑπὲρ θύραν	above a door
ἐν ὄχλῳ	in a crowd

Lesson 10.3

S   V   prep   OP
ἀδελφὸς λέγει σὺν ἀδελφή.
A brother speaks with a sister.

adj   S   V prep adj   OP
ἀγαθὸς ἀδελφὸς λέγει σὺν ἄλλη ἀδελφή.
A good brother speaks with an other sister.

adj   S   V adj DO
ἀγαθὸς ἀδελφὸς γράφει ἄλλα βιβλία.
A good brother writes other books.

S   V   DO   poss
ἀπόστολοι γράφουσι ἀλήθειαν τοῦ θεοῦ.
Apostles write God's truth (truth of God).

S   V prep OP
τέκνα μένουσι ἐν ὄχλῳ.
Children remain in a crowd.

Lesson 10.4

εἰμί	I am	ἐσμέν	we are
εἶ	you (s) are	ἐστέ	you are
ἐστί	he is	εἰσί	they are

adj   S V DO
πίστοι ἀπόστολοι ἐκβάλλουσι δαιμόνια.
Faithful apostles cast out demons.

S   poss V prep OP
ἀδελφαὶ δούλων βαίνουσιν εἰς χώραν.
Sisters of slaves go into a country.

S   V prep OP
υἱὸς βαίνει διὰ θύρας.
A son goes through a door.

S V prep OP V DO
υἱὸς βαίνει διὰ θύρας καὶ βλέπει πέτραν.
A son goes through a door and sees a rock.

S V prep OP
βιβλία εἰσὶν ὑπὸ πέτρας.
Books are under rocks.

Lesson 10.5

Textbook:
What does the man teach the slave?
> *The man teaches the slave about the field and about the rocks.*
How many rocks does the slave throw out of the field?
> *The slave throws ten rocks out of the field.*
Does the man like the slave's work?
> *Yes. The slave does good work, and he has honor.*

Workbook:

	Gender	Number	Case	translation
τῆ ἀρχῆ	F	S	D	the beginning
τὸν δοῦλον	N	S	A	the slave
τὴν τιμήν	F	S	A	(the) honor

Lesson 11.1

ἡ ἔρημος	the desert
ἡ ὁδός	the way
κατά *(w/ gen)*	against
παρά *(w/ gen)*	from
παρί *(w/ gen)*	about

Lesson 11.2

ἀναβαίνω	I go up	ἀναβαίνομεν	we go up
ἀναβαίνεις	you go up	ἀναβαίνετε	you go up
ἀναβαίνει	he goes up	ἀναβαίνουσι	they go up

ἐσθίω	I eat	ἐσθίομεν	we eat
ἐσθίεις	you (s) eat	ἐσθίετε	you eat
ἐσθίει	he eats	ἐσθίουσι	they eat

Lesson 11.3

ἄνθρωπος	ἄνθρωποι
ἀνθρώπου	ἀνθρώπων
ἀνθρώπῳ	ἀνθρώποις
ἄνθρωπον	ἀνθρώπους

δῶρον	δῶρα
δώρου	δώρων
δώρῳ	δώροις
δῶρον	δῶρα

ἀλήθεια	ἀλήθειαι
ἀληθείας	ἀληθειῶν
ἀληθείᾳ	ἀληθείαις
ἀλήθειαν	ἀληθείας

ὁ λίθος	τόν λίθον
ἡ ἀλήθεια	ταῖς ἀληθείαις
τό τέκνον	τῶν τέκνων
ὁ ἄνθρωπος	τοῦ ἀνθρώπου
τό πρόσωπον	τά πρόσωπα

Lesson 11.4

	Singular		
Nom.	ὁ	ἡ	τό
Gen.	τοῦ	τῆς	τοῦ
Dat.	τῷ	τῇ	τῷ
Acc.	τόν	τήν	τό
	Plural		
Nom.	οἱ	αἱ	τά
Gen.	τῶν	τῶν	τῶν
Dat.	τοῖς	ταῖς	τοῖς
Acc.	τούς	τάς	τά

	Singular		
Nom.	δεύτερος	δευτέρα	δεύτερον
Gen.	δευτέρου	δευτέρας	δευτέρου
Dat.	δευτέρῳ	δευτέρᾳ	δευτέρῳ
Acc.	δεύτερον	δευτέραν	δεύτερον
	Plural		
Nom.	δεύτεροι	δεύτεραι	δεύτερα
Gen.	δευτέρων	δευτέρων	δευτέρων
Dat.	δευτέροις	δευτέραις	δευτέροις
Acc.	δευτέρους	δευτέρας	δεύτερα

art   S   V   prep art   OP
ὁ κύριος ἀναβαίνει εἰς τούς οὐρανούς.
The lord goes up into the heavens.

art   S   art poss   V   prep
ὁ κύριος τοῦ κόσμου ἀναβαίνει εἰς
art   OP
τούς οὐρανούς.
The lord of the world goes up into the heavens.

art S   V   art   DO
ὁ θεὸς ἄρχει τῶν ἀγγέλων.[2]
God rules the angels.

art adj   S   V   prep art
οἱ καλοὶ διδάσκαλοι διδάσκουσι σὺν τοῖς
OP
ἀποστόλοις.
The good teachers teach with the apostles.

art adj   S   art   poss
οἱ καλοὶ διδάσκαλοι τῆς ἀληθείας
V   prep art   OP
διδάσκουσι σὺν τοῖς ἀποστόλοις.
The good teachers of the truth teach with the apostles.

Lesson 11.5

1. ἐν
2. σύν
3. εἰς
4. ὑπό
5. ὑπέρ

Lesson 12.1

ἀπό (w/ gen)	from
διά (w/ gen)	through
ἐκ / ἐξ (w/ gen)	out of
μετά (w/ gen)	with
κατά (w/ gen)	against

Lesson 12.2

πείθω	I persuade	πείθομεν	we persuade
πείθεις	you persuade	πείθετε	you persuade
πείθει	he persuades	πείθουσι	they persuade

---

[2] The verb ἄρχω takes the genitive case for its direct object. Most verbs take the accusative case, but you will notice differences in the direct objects of a few verbs here and there. ἄρχω is one of these verbs. If you think of ἄρχω as meaning "I am ruler" then it makes sense for it to take a genitive case: "I am ruler of the servants." (ἄρχω τῶν δουλων.)

κηρύσσω	I bring	κηρύσσομεν	we bring
κηρύσσεις	you bring	κηρύσσετε	you bring
κηρύσσει	he brings	κηρύσσουσι	they bring

negate		translate
οὐ	πείθει	he does not pursuade
οὐκ	ἐσθίω	I do not eat
οὐ	θέλομεν	we do not wish
οὐχ	ἁμαρτάνουσι	they do not sin
οὐκ	ἀναβαίνετε	you do not go up

Lesson 12.3

S   adv   V
They do not eat.
οὐκ ἐσθίουσιν.

S   adv   V   DO
They do not eat bread.
οὐκ ἐσθίουσιν ἄρτον.

art   S   adv   V   DO
The angels do not eat bread.
οἱ ἄγγελοι οὐκ ἐσθίουσιν ἄρτον.

S   adv   V
They do not sin.
οὐχ ἁμαρτάνουσιν.

S   adv   V   prep   OP
They do not sin against God.
οὐχ ἁμαρτάνουσι κατὰ τοῦ θεοῦ.

Week 12.4

	Singular		
Nom.	ὁ	ἡ	τό
Gen.	τοῦ	τῆς	τοῦ
Dat.	τῷ	τῇ	τῷ
Acc.	τόν	τήν	τό
	Plural		
Nom.	οἱ	αἱ	τά
Gen.	τῶν	τῶν	τῶν
Dat.	τοῖς	ταῖς	τοῖς
Acc.	τούς	τάς	τά

	Singular		
Nom.	κακός	κακή	κακόν
Gen.	κακοῦ	κακῆς	κακοῦ
Dat.	κακῷ	κακῇ	κακῷ
Acc.	κακόν	κακήν	κακόν
	Plural		
Nom.	κακοί	κακαί	κακά
Gen.	κακῶν	κακῶν	κακῶν
Dat.	κακοῖς	κακαῖς	κακοῖς
Acc.	κακούς	κακάς	κακά

art adj S   adv   V   art
ὁ ἅγιος ἀπόστολος οὐκ ἀκούει τοὺς
DO
δούλους.
The holy apostle does not hear the slaves.

art adj S   adv   V   art
ὁ ἅγιος ἀπόστολος οὐκ ἀκούει τοὺς
adj DO
κακοὺς δούλους.
The holy apostle does not hear the bad slaves.

art   S   adv   V   prep art   OP
ὁ διδάσκαλος οὐ πάσχει μετὰ τῶν τέκνων.
The teacher does not suffer with the children.

art   S   adv   V   art   DO prep art
ὁ διδάσκαλος οὐκ ἄγει τοὺς υἱοὺς εἰς τὴν
OP
ἔρημον.
The teacher does not lead the sons into the desert.

art   S   poss   adv   V   art
οἱ διδάσκαλοι εὐαγγελίου οὐ λέγουσι τοὺς
adj DO
κακοὺς λόγους.
The teachers of the gospel do not say the bad words.

Lesson 12.5

	φ		α	δ	ε	
	ο	υ		ν	ι	σ
		λ		α	κ	θ
κ	α	τ	α	β	α	ι	ν	ω
η	κ		ι	α	ι	ο	π
ρ	η		ρ	ι	ο		ε
υ		α	ω	ν	υ		ι
σ		ρ		ω	σ		θ
σ		χ			υ		ω
ω		ω		ν			
				η			

Lesson 13.1

δίκαιος	righteous
νεκρός	dead
δεύτερος	second
ὁ Φαρισαῖος	the Pharisee
ἀποστέλλω	I send

Lesson 13.2

αἴρω	I take up (take away)	αἴρομεν	we take up
αἴρεις	you (s) take up	αἴρετε	you take up
αἴρει	he takes up	αἴρουσι	they take up

εἰμί	I am	ἐσμέν	we are
εἶ	you (s) are	ἐστέ	you are
ἐστί	he is	εἰσί	they are

	number	case	translation
ἐγώ	S	N	I
ἡμῖν	P	D	to us
με	S	A	me
μου	S	G	of me
ἡμεῖς	P	N	we

Lesson 13.3

ἄνθρωπος	ἄνθρωποι
ἀνθρώπου	ἀνθρώπων
ἀνθρώπῳ	ἀνθρώποις
ἄνθρωπον	ἀνθρώπους

δῶρον	δῶρα
δώρου	δώρων
δώρῳ	δώροις
δῶρον	δῶρα

ἀλήθεια	ἀλήθειαι
ἀληθείας	ἀληθειῶν
ἀληθείᾳ	ἀληθείαις
ἀλήθειαν	ἀληθείας

of me (my)	μου
me	με
us	ὑμᾶς
to us	ὑμῖν
to me	μοι

Lesson 13.4

	Singular		
Nom.	ὁ	ἡ	τό
Gen.	τοῦ	τῆς	τοῦ
Dat.	τῷ	τῇ	τῷ
Acc.	τόν	τήν	τό
	Plural		
Nom.	οἱ	αἱ	τά
Gen.	τῶν	τῶν	τῶν
Dat.	τοῖς	ταῖς	τοῖς
Acc.	τούς	τάς	τά

art S   pro V
ἡ ἀδελφή μου γράφει.
My sister writes.

art S   pro adv V
ἡ ἀδελφή μού οὐ γράφει.
My sister does not write.

art S   pro adv V   prep art
ὁ ἀδελφὸς ἡμῶν οὐ διδάσκει κατὰ τοῦ
   OP
σταυροῦ.
Our brother does not teach against the cross.

art S   V   prep pro/OP
ὁ τυφλὸς ἀναβαίνει σὺν μοι.
The blind man goes up with me.

art adj S   V   prep pro/OP
ὁ ἄλλος τυφλὸς καταβαίνει σὺν ἡμῖν.
The other blind man goes down with us.

Lesson 13.5

Paths will vary, but the order must be correct:
ἐγώ ⇒ μου ⇒ μοι ⇒ με ⇒
ἡμεῖς ⇒ ἡμῶν ⇒ ἡμῖν ⇒ ἡμᾶς

Lesson 14.1

πιστός	faithful
πονηρός	evil
μικρός	small
ἔσχατος	last
καλός	beautiful

Lesson 14.2

ἄρχω	I rule	ἄρχομεν	we rule
ἄρχεις	you (s) rule	ἄρχετε	you rule
ἄρχει	he rules	ἄρχουσι	they rule

ἐκβάλλω	I cast out	ἐκβάλλομεν	we cast out
ἐκβάλλεις	you cast out	ἐκβάλλετε	you cast out
ἐκβάλλει	he casts out	ἐκβάλλουσι	they cast out

εἰμί	I am	ἐσμέν	we are
εἶ	you (s) are	ἐστέ	you are
ἐστί	he is	εἰσί	they are

	singular		plural	
Nom.	εγώ	I	ἡμεῖς	we
Gen.	μου	of me (mine)	ἡμῶν	of us (our)
Dat.	μοι	to me	ἡμῖν	to us
Acc.	με	me	ἡμᾶς	us

Lesson 14.3

ἄνθρωπος	ἄνθρωποι
ἀνθρώπου	ἀνθρώπων
ἀνθρώπῳ	ἀνθρώποις
ἄνθρωπον	ἀνθρώπους

δῶρον	δῶρα
δώρου	δώρων
δώρῳ	δώροις
δῶρον	δῶρα

ἀλήθεια	ἀλήθειαι
ἀληθείας	ἀληθειῶν
ἀληθείᾳ	ἀληθείαις
ἀλήθειαν	ἀληθείας

	singular		plural	
Nom.	εγώ	I	ἡμεῖς	we
Gen.	μου	of me (mine)	ἡμῶν	of us (our)
Dat.	μοι	to me	ἡμῖν	to us
Acc.	με	me	ἡμᾶς	us

The genitive, accusative, and dative singular cases for the pronoun *I* have special forms when they come after a preposition. These forms are called the emphatic forms. To make these pronouns emphatic, we add an epsilon to the beginning of the word and an accent.

out of me	κατὰ μου
with us	μεθ' ἡμῶν or σὺν ἡμῖν
through us	δι' ἡμῶν
into us	εἰς ἡμᾶς
about me	περὶ μου

Lesson 14.4

	Singular		
Nom.	ὁ	ἡ	τό
Gen.	τοῦ	τῆς	τοῦ
Dat.	τῷ	τῇ	τῷ
Acc.	τόν	τήν	τό
	Plural		
Nom.	οἱ	αἱ	τά
Gen.	τῶν	τῶν	τῶν
Dat.	τοῖς	ταῖς	τοῖς
Acc.	τούς	τάς	τά

	singular		plural	
Nom.	εγώ	I	ἡμεῖς	we
Gen.	μου	of me (mine)	ἡμῶν	of us (our)
Dat.	μοι	to me	ἡμῖν	to us
Acc.	με	me	ἡμᾶς	us

art   S   V   prep   OP
ὁ ἄνθρωπος βαίνει μετ' ἐμοῦ.
The man goes with me.

art   S   V   prep   OP
ὁ τυφλὸς ἐσθίει σὺν ἡμῖν.
The blind man eats with me.

art   S   art   S   pro   V
ὁ τυφλὸς καὶ ἡ ἀδελφή μου καταβαίνουσι
prep   OP
μετ' ἐμοῦ.
The blind man and the sister of me (my sister) go down with me.

art   S   pro   V   art   DO
ὁ διδάσκαλος ἡμῶν διδάσκει τὴν σοφίαν.
The teacher of us (Our teacher) teaches the
wisdom.

art   adj   S   pro   V   art   DO
ὁ πιστὸς κύριος ἡμῶν ἄρχει τοῦ ὄχλου.
The faithful lord of us (Our faithful lord) rules the
crowd.

Lesson 15.1

ἄρχω	I rule
καταβαίνω	I go up
ἐσθίω	I eat
πείθω	I persuade
ἡ δικαιοσύνη	the righteousness
ἐγώ	I
ἀμήν	verily, truly, amen
ὁ χρόνος	the time
ἡ συναγωγή	the synagogue
τό σημεῖον	the sign
ἀναβαίνω	I go up
αἴρω	I take up/away
κηρύσσω	I preach
ἡ φυλακή	the prison
οὐ	not
σύ	you
μόνος	alone, only
ἡ γῆ	the earth
ἡ ἐξουσία	the power
ἡ σοφία	the wisdom

Lesson 15.2

πείθω	I persuade		πείθομεν	we persuade
πείθεις	you persuade		πείθετε	you persuade
πείθει	he persuades		πείθουσι	they persuade

κηρύσσω	I bring		κηρύσσομεν	we bring
κηρύσσεις	you bring		κηρύσσετε	you bring
κηρύσσει	he brings		κηρύσσουσι	they bring

εἰμί	I am		ἐσμέν	we are
εἶ	you (s) are		ἐστέ	you are
ἐστί	he is		εἰσί	they are

	singular		plural	
Nom.	ἐγώ	I	ἡμεῖς	we
Gen.	μου	of me (mine)	ἡμῶν	of us (our)
Dat.	μοι	to me	ἡμῖν	to us
Acc.	με	me	ἡμᾶς	us

οὐ	...	<u>consonants</u>
οὐκ	...	<u>vowels with smooth breathing marks</u>
οὐχ	...	<u>vowels with rough breathing marks</u>

negate		translate
<u>οὐ</u>	λέγει	he does not read
<u>οὐκ</u>	ἐκβάλλουσι	they do not castout
<u>οὐχ</u>	ἁμαρτάνουσι	they do not sin
<u>οὐ</u>	διδάσκεις	you do not teach
<u>οὐκ</u>	ἀναβαίνετε	you do not go up

Lesson 15.3

ἄνθρωπος		ἄνθρωποι
ἀνθρώπου		ἀνθρώπων
ἀνθρώπῳ		ἀνθρώποις
ἄνθρωπον		ἀνθρώπους

δῶρον		δῶρα
δώρου		δώρων
δώρῳ		δώροις
δῶρον		δῶρα

ἀλήθεια		ἀλήθειαι
ἀληθείας		ἀληθειῶν
ἀληθείᾳ		ἀληθείαις
ἀλήθειαν		ἀληθείας

prep art   OP   S   V   DO
ἐν τῷ Χριστῷ ἡμεῖς ἔχομεν ζωήν.
In Christ we have life.

art   S   pro   adv   V   prep art   OP
ἡ οἰκία ἡμῶν οὐκ ἐστιν ἐν τῇ ἐρήμῳ.
The house of us (our house) is not in the desert.

art   S   ἄνθρωποι   V   prep art
οἱ ἄνθρωποι κηρύσσουσι περὶ τῆς
OP   art   poss
ἐξουσίας τοῦ θεοῦ.
The men preach about the power of God.

V   pro   V   pro
κηρύσσουσί μοι καὶ πείθουσί με.
They preach to me and persuade me.

adv   V   art   DO
οὐ πείθουσι τὰ δαιμόνια.
They do not persuade the demons.

Lesson 15.4

	Singular		
Nom.	ὁ	ἡ	τό
Gen.	τοῦ	τῆς	τοῦ
Dat.	τῷ	τῇ	τῷ
Acc.	τόν	τήν	τό
	Plural		
Nom.	οἱ	αἱ	τά
Gen.	τῶν	τῶν	τῶν
Dat.	τοῖς	ταῖς	τοῖς
Acc.	τούς	τάς	τά

S   V   art   DO
We see the books.
ἡμεῖς βλέπομεν τὰ βιβλία.

S   V   pro   DO
We see our books.
ἡμεῖς βλέπομεν τὰ βιβλία ἡμῶν.

S   V   art   DO   prep   OP
I bring the books with me.
ἐγὼ φέρω τὰ βιβλία μετὰ μου (*or* σὺν μοι).

S   V   prep   OP
We preach about God.
ἡμεῖς κηρύσσομεν περὶ θεοῦ.

S   adv   V   prep   OP
Demons do not preach about God.
τὰ δαιμόνια οὐ κηρύσσουσι περὶ θεοῦ.

Lesson 15.5

Textbook:
Where is the man who preaches?
The man who preaches is in prison.
What do faithful men have in their hearts?
Faithful men have wisdom in their hearts.
How does the man persuade the Pharisee?
The man persuades the Pharisee with words and signs.
Where does the man get his power?
He gets his power from God.

Lesson 16.1

ἀγαθός	good (moral)
καλός	beautiful
ἄλλος	other
ἔσχατος	last
κακός	bad

Lesson 16.2

πίπτω	πίπτομεν	εἰμί	ἐσμέν
πίπτεις	πίπτετε	εἶ	ἐστέ
πίπτει	πίπτουσι	ἐστί	εἰσί

...but he writes   γράφει δέ
...but the angel believes   ὁ δὲ ἄγγελος
    πιστεύει.
...but the wisdom remains   ἡ δὲ σοφία μένει.

Lesson 16.3

ἄνθρωπος	ἄνθρωποι
ἀνθρώπου	ἀνθρώπων
ἀνθρώπῳ	ἀνθρώποις
ἄνθρωπον	ἀνθρώπους

δῶρον	δῶρα
δώρου	δώρων
δώρῳ	δώροις
δῶρον	δῶρα

ἀλήθεια	ἀλήθειαι
ἀληθείας	ἀληθειῶν
ἀληθείᾳ	ἀληθείαις
ἀλήθειαν	ἀληθείας

art   S   V   con art S   adv
ὁ διδάσκαλος διδάσκει ἀλλὰ ὁ ὄχλος οὐκ
V
ἀκούει.
The teacher teaches but the crowd does not hear.

con V (S) art DO   V (S)   adj
εἰ διδάσκει τὸν δοῦλον, ἐστὶν ἀγαθὸς
(predicate nominative)
ἄνθρωπος.
If he teaches the slave, he is a good man.

V (S)   con   S   V   adj (predicate nominative)
λέγομεν ὅτι θεός ἐστιν ἀγαθός.
We say that God is good.

art S V adj art con S V
ὁ υἱός ἐστι καλός, ὁ δὲ ἀδελφός ἐστι
adj
κακός.

The son is good, but the brother is bad.
con V (S) DO V (S)
ὅτι ἔχεις σοφίαν, διδάσκεις.
Because you have wisdom, you teach.

Lesson 16.4

	Singular		
Nom.	ὁ	ἡ	τό
Gen.	τοῦ	τῆς	τοῦ
Dat.	τῷ	τῇ	τῷ
Acc.	τόν	τήν	τό
	Plural		
Nom.	οἱ	αἱ	τά
Gen.	τῶν	τῶν	τῶν
Dat.	τοῖς	ταῖς	τοῖς
Acc.	τούς	τάς	τά

	singular		plural	
Nom.	εγώ	I	ἡμεῖς	we
Gen.	μου	of me (mine)	ἡμῶν	of us (our)
Dat.	μοι	to me	ἡμῖν	to us
Acc.	με	me	ἡμᾶς	us

art S V con S V adj
The men say that God is good.
οἱ ἄνθρωποι λέγουσιν ὅτι θεός ἐστιν
ἀγαθός.
(Both verbs in this sentence take the movable nu, because the words following them begin with vowels.)

art S adv V prep art OP con
The brothers do not go into the house because
S V prep art OP
they preach in the field.
οἱ ἀδελφοὶ οὐ βαίνουσιν εἰς τὸν οἶκον
(τὴν οἰκίαν) ὅτι κηρύσσουσιν ἐν τῷ
ἀγρῷ.

art S V adj con S V art DO
The promise is good, and they believe[3] the promise.
ἡ ἐπαγγελία ἐστὶν ἀγαθή (καλή),
πιστεύουσι δὲ τῇ ἐπαγγελίᾳ.
(Possibly, the student used καὶ for the word 'and' in this sentence. This would be grammatically correct, but take the opportunity to show the student this construction, using the postpositive δὲ.)

art S V art DO con S adv
The sinner hears the gospel, but he does not
V
believe.
ὁ ἁμαρτωλὸς ἀκούει τὸ εὐαγγέλιον, ἀλλὰ
οὐ πιστεύει.

art S _V_ con art S _V_
The sister goes up, but the brother goes down.
ἡ ἀδελφὴ ἀναβαίνει, ὁ δὲ ἀδελφὸς
καταβαίνει.

Lesson 17.1

ἐγώ	I
καλύπτω	I hide
ἡ οἰκία	the house
ὁ καρπός	the fruit
ὁ Χριστός	the Christ

Lesson 17.2

ἀνοίγω	ἀνοίγομεν	σπείρω	σπείρομεν
ἀνοίγεις	ἀνοίγετε	σπείρεις	σπείρετε
ἀνοίγει	ἀνοίγουσι	σπείρει	σπείρουσι

σὺν ὑμῖν	with you
μοι	to me
ὑμῶν	of you/your
ἡμῖν	to us
σύ	you
ὑπὲρ ἐμέ	above me
σέ	you
καθ᾽ ὑμῶν	against you
ὑμεῖς	you
περὶ σοῦ	about you

---

[3] Like ἄρχω, πιστεύω also takes its direct object in a case other than the accusative. Πιστεύω takes the **dative case**.

Lesson 17.3

ἄνθρωπος	ἄνθρωποι
ἀνθρώπου	ἀνθρώπων
ἀνθρώπῳ	ἀνθρώποις
ἄνθρωπον	ἀνθρώπους

δῶρον	δῶρα
δώρου	δώρων
δώρῳ	δώροις
δῶρον	δῶρα

ἀλήθεια	ἀλήθειαι
ἀληθείας	ἀληθειῶν
ἀληθείᾳ	ἀληθείαις
ἀλήθειαν	ἀληθείας

	singular		plural	
Nom.	σύ	you	ὑμεῖς	you
Gen.	σοῦ	of you (your)	ὑμῶν	of you (your)
Dat.	σοί	to you	ὑμῖν	to you
Acc.	σέ	you	ὑμᾶς	you

S   V   art   DO
σὺ ἀνοίγεις τὴν θύραν.
You open the door.

art   S   V   adv   DO con DO
ὁ ἀπόστολος ἐλέγχει πάλιν σὲ καὶ με.
The apostle rebukes you and me again.

   V (S)   prep   OP/pro
ἀναβαίνομεν μεθ᾽ ὑμῶν.
We go up with you.

   V (S)   prep   OP/pro con
ἀναβαίνομεν μεθ᾽ ὑμῶν ὅτι
   V (S)   art DO   prep OP/pro
παραλαμβάνομεν τὸν λόγον ἀπ᾽ ὑμῶν.
We go up with you because we receive the word from you.

art   S   V   adv   DO con DO
ὁ ἀπόστολος ἐλέγχει πάλιν σὲ καὶ με,
S   con adv   V
ἡμεῖς δὲ οὐκ ἀκούομεν.
The apostle rebukes you and me again, but we do not hear.

Lesson 17.4

	Singular		
Nom.	ὁ	ἡ	τό
Gen.	τοῦ	τῆς	τοῦ
Dat.	τῷ	τῇ	τῷ
Acc.	τόν	τήν	τό
	Plural		
Nom.	οἱ	αἱ	τά
Gen.	τῶν	τῶν	τῶν
Dat.	τοῖς	ταῖς	τοῖς
Acc.	τούς	τάς	τά

	Singular		
Nom.	δίκαιος	δικαία	δίκαιον
Gen.	δικαίου	δικαίας	δικαίου
Dat.	δικαίῳ	δικαίᾳ	δικαίῳ
Acc.	δίκαιον	δικαίαν	δίκαιον
	Plural		
Nom.	δίκαιοι	δίκαιαι	δίκαια
Gen.	δικαίων	δικαίων	δικαίων
Dat.	δικαίοις	δικαίαις	δικαίοις
Acc.	δικαίους	δικαίας	δίκαια

	Singular		
Nom.	ἀγαθός	ἀγαθή	ἀγαθόν
Gen.	ἀγαθοῦ	ἀγαθῆς	ἀγαθοῦ
Dat.	ἀγαθῷ	ἀγαθῇ	ἀγαθῷ
Acc.	ἀγαθόν	ἀγαθήν	ἀγαθόν
	Plural		
Nom.	ἀγαθοί	ἀγαθαί	ἀγαθά
Gen.	ἀγαθῶν	ἀγαθῶν	ἀγαθῶν
Dat.	ἀγαθοῖς	ἀγαθαῖς	ἀγαθοῖς
Acc.	ἀγαθούς	ἀγαθάς	ἀγαθά

S   V   DO/pro adv   con adv
You rebuke me   again and again.
σὺ ἐλέγκεις με πάλιν καὶ πάλιν.

art   __S__   V   DO prep OP/pro
The blind man receives gifts from you (s).
ὁ τυφλὸς παραλαμβάνει δῶρα παρά [ἀπό] σου.

S V   con art   S   adv V DO/pro
I speak, but the crowd does not hear me.
ἐγώ, ὁ δὲ ὄχλος οὐκ ἀκούει με.

S   V   art   DO   con   S   V   art   DO
We open the door because we hear the men.
ἡμεῖς ἀνοίγομεν τὴν θύραν ὅτι ἀκούομεν
τοὺς ἀνθρώπους.

art   S   prep   OP/pro   V   prep art   OP
The son of you (your son) sows in the field.
ὁ υἱὸς σου σπείρει ἐν τῷ ἀγρῷ.

Lesson 18.1

ἡ ἐπαγγελία	the promise
ἡ χαρά	the joy
θέλω	I wish
ἁμαρτάνω	I sin
ὁ Ἰουδαῖος	the Jew

Lesson 18.2

κρίνω	I judge		κρίνομεν	we judge
κρίνεις	you judge		κρίνετε	you judge
κρίνει	he judges		κρίνουσι	they judge

ἐλέγχω	I rebuke		ἐλέγχομεν	we rebuke
ἐλέγχεις	you rebuke		ἐλέγχετε	you rebuke
ἐλέγχει	he rebukes		ἐλέγχουσι	they rebuke

Lesson 18.3

ἄνθρωπος	ἄνθρωποι
ἀνθρώπου	ἀνθρώπων
ἀνθρώπῳ	ἀνθρώποις
ἄνθρωπον	ἀνθρώπους

δῶρον	δῶρα
δώρου	δώρων
δώρῳ	δώροις
δῶρον	δῶρα

ἀλήθεια	ἀλήθειαι
ἀληθείας	ἀληθειῶν
ἀληθείᾳ	ἀληθείαις
ἀλήθειαν	ἀληθείας

	Gender	Number	Case	translation
πρόβατα	N	P	N/A	sheep
φαρισαίου	M	S	G	of a pharisee
χαρῶν	F	P	G	of joys
τόπῳ	M	S	D	to/for a place
ἡλίοις	M	P	D	to/for suns
δήμου	M	S	G	of a people

γάμων	M	P	G	of marriages
ζωαῖς	F	P	D	to/for lives
ὁδόν	F	S	A	way

(remember ἡ ὁδός is a feminine noun that takes masculine endings)

| καρδίαν | F | S | A | heart |

Lesson 18.4

	singular		plural	
Nom.	εγώ	I	ἡμεῖς	we
Gen.	μου	of me (mine)	ἡμῶν	of us (our)
Dat.	μοι	to me	ἡμῖν	to us
Acc.	με	me	ἡμᾶς	us

	singular		plural	
Nom.	σύ	you	ὑμεῖς	you
Gen.	σοῦ	of you (your)	ὑμῶν	of you (your)
Dat.	σοί	to you	ὑμῖν	to you
Acc.	σέ	you	ὑμᾶς	you

art   S   V   art   DO   poss
οἱ ἀπόστολοι κηρύσσουσι τὸν λόγον θεοῦ
art   Dat
τῷ δήμῳ.
The apostles preach the Word of God to the people.

art   D   art   poss   V   art
ἡ καρδία τῆς ἀδελφῆς γινώσκει τὴν
                              DO
ἀλήθειαν.
The heart of the sister knows the truth.

V (S)   DO   art   Dat   poss/pro
γράφω λόγους τῷ υἱῷ μου.
I write words to my son.

V (S)   DO   prep   OP   art   Dat   poss/pro
γράφω λόγους περὶ θεοῦ τῷ ἀδελφῷ σου.
I write words about God to your brother.

V (S)   art   adj   DO   prep   art
βλέπομεν τὸν καλὸν ἥλιον ἐν τοῖς
                                    OP
οὐρανοῖς.
We see the beautiful sun in the heavens.

Lesson 18.5

```
|   | β λ ε π ω |
| κ | α |           | α |
σ | η | λ |         | ν |   | π
π α ρ α λ α μ β α ν ο μ ε ν
ε | υ | ε | ε |     | ι | ι
ι | σ | ι | ν |     | γ | θ
ρ | σ | ε | α | ε | ο
ε | ε | υ | τ | ρ | ι | μ
τ | ι | ε λ ε γ χ ω | ε
ε ς λ | ο |   | μ ε ν ω
    | ε |   | υ
λ ε χ ε ι | ε ι σ ι
    | ς |   | ι
```

Lesson 19.1

ἡ φωνή	the voice
ἡ ψυχή	the soul / life
ἡ καρδία	the heart
ἡ ἀγάπη	the love
ἡ ἁμαρτία	the sin

Lesson 19.2

θέλω	θέλομεν	εἰμί	ἐσμέν
θέλεις	θέλετε	εἶ	ἐστέ
θέλει	θέλουσι	ἐστί	εἰσί

	Singular		
Nom.	ὁ	ἡ	τό
Gen.	τοῦ	τῆς	τοῦ
Dat.	τῷ	τῇ	τῷ
Acc.	τόν	τήν	τό
	Plural		
Nom.	οἱ	αἱ	τά
Gen.	τῶν	τῶν	τῶν
Dat.	τοῖς	ταῖς	τοῖς
Acc.	τούς	τάς	τά

	Singular		
Nom.	ἄλλος	ἄλλη	ἄλλον
Gen.	ἄλλου	ἄλλης	ἄλλου
Dat.	ἄλλῳ	ἄλλη	ἄλλῳ
Acc.	ἄλλον	ἄλλην	ἄλλον
	Plural		
Nom.	ἄλλοι	ἄλλαι	ἄλλα
Gen.	ἄλλων	ἄλλων	ἄλλων
Dat.	ἄλλοις	ἄλλαις	ἄλλοις
Acc.	ἄλλους	ἄλλας	ἄλλα

hearts (nominative)	καρδίαι
to/for a village	κώμη
of a testimony	μαρτυρίας
to/for souls	ψυχαῖς
eye (accusative)	ὀφθαλμόν
of sheep (plural)	προβάτων
Pharisee (nominative)	Φαρισαιος
to/for a sun	ἡλίῳ
weddings (accusative)	γάμους
of salvation	σωτηρίας

Lesson 19.3

ἄνθρωπος		ἄνθρωποι
ἀνθρώπου		ἀνθρώπων
ἀνθρώπῳ		ἀνθρώποις
ἄνθρωπον		ἀνθρώπους

δῶρον		δῶρα
δώρου		δώρων
δώρῳ		δώροις
δῶρον		δῶρα

ἀλήθεια		ἀλήθειαι
ἀληθείας		ἀληθειῶν
ἀληθείᾳ		ἀληθείαις
ἀλήθειαν		ἀληθείας

art   S   V   art   DO prep art   OP
ὁ κύριος ἄγει τὸν δῆμον εἰς τὴν βασιλείαν.
The lord leads the people into the kingdom.

V (S)   art   DO   poss   IO
λέγομεν τοὺς λόγους ἀληθείας δούλοις.
We speak the words of truth to the slaves.

```
art        S          V      prep art   OP
ὁ ἄνθρωπος καλύπτει ἐν τῷ σταδίῳ.
The man hides in the stadium.

art     S         V       DO    con   DO
τὰ τέκνα ἐσθίουσιν ἄρτον καὶ καρπόν.
The child eats bread and fruit.

art    S        V    art    DO    prep art   OP
ὁ κύριος σώζει τὸν τυφλόν ἐν τῇ κώμῃ
prep   art      OP
ἀπὸ τῶν δαιμονίων.
The lord saves the blind man in the village from
the demons.
```

Lesson 19.4

	singular		plural	
Nom.	εγώ	I	ἡμεῖς	we
Gen.	μου	of me (mine)	ἡμῶν	of us (our)
Dat.	μοι	to me	ἡμῖν	to us
Acc.	με	me	ἡμᾶς	us

	singular		plural	
Nom.	σύ	you	ὑμεῖς	you
Gen.	σοῦ	of you (your)	ὑμῶν	of you (your)
Dat.	σοί	to you	ὑμῖν	to you
Acc.	σέ	you	ὑμᾶς	you

```
S     V  art  DO    poss
We hear the words of truth.
ἀκούομεν τοὺς λόγους ἀληθείας.

art    S   V   art  DO    poss
The eye sees the work of men.
ὁ ὀφθαλμὸς βλέπει τὸ ἐργον ἀνθρώπων.

poss/pro  S    (art  S  poss/pro) V art  DO
Our      eyes (the eyes  of us) see the work of
    adj     poss
faithful men.
οἱ ὀφθαλμοὶ ἡμῶν βλέπουσι τὸ ἐργον
πιστων ἀνθρώπων.
```

```
art    S      V   adj    DO       art  IO
The teacher says good words to the child.
ὁ διδασκαλος λέγει ἀγαθοὺς [καλοὺς]
λόγους τῷ τέκνῳ.

art    S     V   art DO  prep art  OP
The servant leads the sheep out of the village.
ὁ δοῦλος ἄγει τὸ πρόβατον ἐκ τῆς κώμης.
```

Lesson 19.5

martyr	ἡ μαρτυρία	the testimony
monologue		
monotone	μόνος	alone, only
chronology	ὁ χρόνος	the time
ophthalmologist	ὁ ὀφθαλμός	the eye
petrified	ἡ πέτρα	the rock
helium	ὁ ἥλιος	the sun

Lesson 20.1

ἀλλά	but
εἰ	if
ὅτι	because, that
+δέ	but
ἀνοίγω	I open
ἐλέγχω	I rebuke
σπείρω	I sow
παραλαμβάνω	I receive
πάλιν	again
τό πρόβατον	the sheep
ὁ ἥλιος	the sun
᾽Αβραάμ	Abraham
ὁ δῆμος	the people
ὁ γάμος	the wedding
ἡ μαρτυρία	the testimony
ὁ οφθαλμός	the eye
τό στάδιον	the stadium
ἡ κώμη	the village
ἡ σωτηρία	the salvation
ἡ σοφία	the wisdom

Lesson 20.2

ἀνοίγω	ἀνοίγομεν	σπείρω	σπείρομεν
ἀνοίγεις	ἀνοίγετε	σπείρεις	σπείρετε
ἀνοίγει	ἀνοίγουσι	σπείρει	σπείρουσι

Conjunctions __join (or connect)__ words, phrases, or thoughts.

A *postpositive* may not be the __first__ word in a Greek sentence or phrase.

The three forms of the adverb "not" are __οὐ__ , __οὐχ,__ and __οὐκ__ .

ἀκούω τοὺς λόγους οὐ δὲ βλέπω τὸν ἄνθρωπον. ὁ ἄνθρωπος λέγει τοὺς λόγους ὅτι οἱ λόγοι ἀνοίγουσι τὴν θύραν ἀληθείας. παραλαμβάνομεν τὴν ἀλήθειαν καὶ ἡ ἀλήθειά ἐστιν ἀγαθή.

I hear the words but I do not see the man. The man says the words because the words open the door of truth. We receive the truth and the truth is good.

Lesson 20.3

ἄνθρωπος	ἄνθρωποι
ἀνθρώπου	ἀνθρώπων
ἀνθρώπῳ	ἀνθρώποις
ἄνθρωπον	ἀνθρώπους

δῶρον	δῶρα
δώρου	δώρων
δώρῳ	δώροις
δῶρον	δῶρα

ἀλήθεια	ἀλήθειαι
ἀληθείας	ἀληθειῶν
ἀληθείᾳ	ἀληθείαις
ἀλήθειαν	ἀληθείας

Genitive   indirect object
Accusative   subject
Dative   possessive
Nominative   direct object

	Gender	Number	Case	translation
σωτηρίαν	F	S	A	salvation
ἡλίου	M	S	G	of a sun
δήμῳ	M	S	D	to/for a people
πρόβατα	N	P	N/A	sheep
ὀφθαλμούς	M	P	A	eyes
γάμων	M	P	G	of weddings
μαρτυρίαις	F	P	D	to/for testimonies
κώμης	F	S	G	of a village

ἡλίον   M   S   A   sun
σωταρία   F   S   D   to/for salvation

Lesson 20.4

	singular		plural	
Nom.	εγώ	I	ἡμεῖς	we
Gen.	μου	of me (mine)	ἡμῶν	of us (our)
Dat.	μοι	to me	ἡμῖν	to us
Acc.	με	me	ἡμᾶς	us

	singular		plural	
Nom.	σύ	you	ὑμεῖς	you
Gen.	σοῦ	of you (your)	ὑμῶν	of you (your)
Dat.	σοί	to you	ὑμῖν	to you
Acc.	σέ	you	ὑμᾶς	you

Πάτερ ἡμῶν ὁ ἐν τοῖς οὐρανοῖς,
ἁγιασθήτω τὸ ὄνομά σου,
ἐλθέτω ἡ βασιλεία σου,
γενηθήτω τὸ θέλημά σου,
ὡς ἐν οὐρανῷ καὶ ἐπὶ τῆς γῆς.
τὸν ἄρτον ἡμῶν τὸν ἐπιούσιον δὸς ἡμῖν
σήμερον.
καὶ ἄφες ἡμῖν τὰ ὀφειλήματα ἡμῶν,
ὡς καὶ ἡμεῖς ἀφίεμεν τοῖς ὀφειλέταις
ἡμῶν.

	Number	Case	translation
ἡμῶν	P	G	of us
σου	S	G	of you
σου	S	G	of you
σου	S	G	of you
ἡμῶν	P	G	of us
ἡμῖν	P	D	to us
ἡμῖν	P	D	to us
ἡμῶν	P	G	of us
ἡμεῖς	P	N	we
ἡμῶν	P	G	of us

Lesson 21.1

ἡ γραφή	the writing
ἡ παραβολή	the parable
ἡ ζωή	the life
ἡ εἰρήνη	the peace
ἡ ἐντολή	the commandment

Lesson 21.2

διώκω	I persecute	διώκομεν	we persecute
διώκεις	you persecute	διώκετε	you persecute
διώκει	he persecutes	διώκουσι	they persecute

κόπτω	I cut	κόπτομεν	we cut
κόπτεις	you cut	κόπτετε	you cut
κόπτει	he cuts	κόπτουσι	they cut

The tutor *was instructing.*
Geese *were chasing* children.
You *were walking* to the park.
We *were eating* dinner.
I *was running* for office.

Lesson 21.3

ἄνθρωπος	ἄνθρωποι
ἀνθρώπου	ἀνθρώπων
ἀνθρώπῳ	ἀνθρώποις
ἄνθρωπον	ἀνθρώπους

δῶρον	δῶρα
δώρου	δώρων
δώρῳ	δώροις
δῶρον	δῶρα

ἀλήθεια	ἀλήθειαι
ἀληθείας	ἀληθειῶν
ἀληθείᾳ	ἀληθείαις
ἀλήθειαν	ἀληθείας

ἔλυον	ἐλύομεν
ἔλυες	ἐλύετε
ἔλυε	ἔλυον

ἔλυον	I was loosing	ἐλύομεν	we were loosing
ἔλυες	you were loosing	ἐλύετε	you were loosing
ἔλυε	he was loosing	ἔλυον	they were loosing

Lesson 21.4

	singular		plural	
Nom.	ἐγώ	I	ἡμεῖς	we
Gen.	μου	of me (mine)	ἡμῶν	of us (our)
Dat.	μοι	to me	ἡμῖν	to us
Acc.	με	me	ἡμᾶς	us

	singular		plural	
Nom.	σύ	you	ὑμεῖς	you
Gen.	σοῦ	of you (your)	ὑμῶν	of you (your)
Dat.	σοί	to you	ὑμῖν	to you
Acc.	σέ	you	ὑμᾶς	you

	Singular		
Nom.	ὁ	ἡ	τό
Gen.	τοῦ	τῆς	τοῦ
Dat.	τῷ	τῇ	τῷ
Acc.	τόν	τήν	τό
	Plural		
Nom.	οἱ	αἱ	τά
Gen.	τῶν	τῶν	τῶν
Dat.	τοῖς	ταῖς	τοῖς
Acc.	τούς	τάς	τά

ἔθελον	I was wishing	ἐθέλομεν	we were wishing
ἔθελες	you were wishing	ἐθέλετε	you were wishing
ἔθελε	he was wishing	ἔθελον	they were wishing

ἐπίπτομεν	we were falling
ἐπίστευες	you were believing
κόπτουσι	they cut
ἔβαινον	I was going / they were going
ἀνοίγεις	you open
ἔσπειρε	he was sowing
ἐκηρύσσετε	you were preaching
πείθει	he persuades
ἐκβάλλω	I cast out
ἐγίνωσκον	I was knowing / they were knowing

Lesson 22.1

	translation	part of speech	nouns only:	
			declension	gender
ἡ ἀλήθεια	the truth	N	1ˢᵗ	F
ἡ ἡμέρα	the day	N	1ˢᵗ	F
ἡ βασιλεία	the kingdom	N	1ˢᵗ	F
ἡ ὥρα	the hour	N	1ˢᵗ	F
ἡ ἐκκλησία	the church	N	1ˢᵗ	F

Lesson 22.2

δοξάζω	I glorify	δοξάζομεν	we glorify
δοξάζεις	you glorify	δοξάζετε	you glorify
δοξάζει	he glorifies	δοξάζουσι	they glorify

ἀποκτείνω	I kill	ἀποκτείνομεν	we kill
ἀποκτείνεις	you kill	ἀποκτείνετε	you kill
ἀποκτείνει	he kills	ἀποκτείνουσι	they kill

εἰμί	I am	ἐσμέν	we are
εἶ	you (s) are	ἐστέ	you are
ἐστί	he is	εἰσί	they are

ἔβαλλον	I was throwing	ἐβάλλομεν	we were throwing
ἔβαλλες	you were throwing	ἐβάλλετε	you were throwing
ἔβαλλε	he was throwing	ἔβαλλον	they were throwing

ἔβαινον	I was going	ἐβαίνομεν	we were going
ἔβαινες	you were going	ἐβαίνετε	you were going
ἔβαινε	he was going	ἔβαινον	they were going

Lesson 22.3

ἄνθρωπος	ἄνθρωποι
ἀνθρώπου	ἀνθρώπων
ἀνθρώπῳ	ἀνθρώποις
ἄνθρωπον	ἀνθρώπους

δῶρον	δῶρα
δώρου	δώρων
δώρῳ	δώροις
δῶρον	δῶρα

ἀλήθεια	ἀλήθειαι
ἀληθείας	ἀληθειῶν
ἀληθείᾳ	ἀληθείαις
ἀλήθειαν	ἀληθείας

ἀνοίγω	→ ἤνοιγον	I was opening
ἄγομεν	→ ἤγομεν	we were leading
διδάσκει	→ ἐδίδασκες	you were teaching
ἄρχετε	→ ἤρχετε	you were ruling
ἐσθίω	→ ἤσθιον	I was eating

Lesson 22.4

	singular		plural	
Nom.	εγώ	I	ἡμεῖς	we
Gen.	μου	of me (mine)	ἡμῶν	of us (our)
Dat.	μοι	to me	ἡμῖν	to us
Acc.	με	me	ἡμᾶς	us

	singular		plural	
Nom.	σύ	you	ὑμεῖς	you
Gen.	σοῦ	of you (your)	ὑμῶν	of you (your)
Dat.	σοί	to you	ὑμῖν	to you
Acc.	σέ	you	ὑμᾶς	you

		Singular	
Nom.	ὁ	ἡ	τό
Gen.	τοῦ	τῆς	τοῦ
Dat.	τῷ	τῇ	τῷ
Acc.	τόν	τήν	τό
		Plural	
Nom.	οἱ	αἱ	τά
Gen.	τῶν	τῶν	τῶν
Dat.	τοῖς	ταῖς	τοῖς
Acc.	τούς	τάς	τά

art S V art DO
οἱ ἄνθρωποι ἐδόξαζον τὸν θεόν.
The men were glorifying God.

V (S) DO
ἠνοίγομεν θύραν.
We were opening a door.

V (S) DO prep art OP
ἠσθίετε ἄρτον ἐν τῷ οἴκῳ.
You were eating bread in the house.

art S V prep art OP
ὁ κύριος ἐκήρυσσεν ἐν τῷ ἱερῷ.
The Lord was preaching in the temple.

art S V DO
τὰ τέκνα ἔβαλλον λίθους.
The children were throwing stones.

Lesson 23.1

	translation	*part of speech*
ὁ ἄρτος	the bread	N
ὁ τυφλός	the blind man	N
σώζω	I save	V
Ἰησοῦς	Jesus	N
βαίνω	I go	V

Lesson 23.2

χαίρω	χαίρομεν	ἔχαιρον	ἐχαίρομεν
χαίρεις	χαίρετε	ἔχαιρες	ἐχαίρετε
χαίρει	χαίρουσι	ἔχαιρε	ἔχαιρον

ἀποθνήσκουσι	→	ἀπέθνησκον
(they die)		they were dying
παραλαμβάνετε	→	παρελαμβάνετε
(you receive)		you were receiving
ἀποστέλλομεν	→	ἀπεστέλλομεν
(we send)		we were sending
καταβαίνεις	→	κατέβαινες
(you go down)		you were going down
ἀποκτείνει	→	ἀπέκτεινε
(he kills)		he was killing

Lesson 23.3

ἄνθρωπος	ἄνθρωποι
ἀνθρώπου	ἀνθρώπων
ἀνθρώπῳ	ἀνθρώποις
ἄνθρωπον	ἀνθρώπους

δῶρον	δῶρα
δώρου	δώρων
δώρῳ	δώροις
δῶρον	δῶρα

ἀλήθεια	ἀλήθειαι
ἀληθείας	ἀληθειῶν
ἀληθείᾳ	ἀληθείαις
ἀλήθειαν	ἀληθείας

art S V art DO art poss
οἱ ἄνθρωποι ἤκουον τὸν λόγον τοῦ θεοῦ.
The men were hearing the word of God.

art S V art DO
τὸ τέκνον ἔβλεπε τοὺς ἀποστόλους.
The child was seeing the apostles.

S V prep art OP
δικαιοσύνη ἐστιν ἀπὸ τοῦ θεοῦ.
Righteousness is from God.

art adj S V art DO poss
ὁ αἰώνιος θεὸς ἔλεγε τοὺς λόγους ζωῆς.
The eternal God was speaking the words of life.

V (S) art DO
ἐκόπτομεν τὸν ἄρτον.
We were cutting the bread.

Lesson 23.4

	singular		*plural*	
Nom.	εγώ	I	ἡμεῖς	we
Gen.	μου	of me (mine)	ἡμῶν	of us (our)
Dat.	μοι	to me	ἡμῖν	to us
Acc.	με	me	ἡμᾶς	us

	singular		*plural*	
Nom.	σύ	you	ὑμεῖς	you
Gen.	σοῦ	of you (your)	ὑμῶν	of you (your)
Dat.	σοί	to you	ὑμῖν	to you
Acc.	σέ	you	ὑμᾶς	you

Singular			
Nom.	ὁ	ἡ	τό
Gen.	τοῦ	τῆς	τοῦ
Dat.	τῷ	τῇ	τῷ
Acc.	τόν	τήν	τό
Plural			
Nom.	οἱ	αἱ	τά
Gen.	τῶν	τῶν	τῶν
Dat.	τοῖς	ταῖς	τοῖς
Acc.	τούς	τάς	τά

The crowd was hearing the Son of God.
ὁ ὄχλος ἤκουε τὸν υἱὸν τοῦ θεοῦ.

The crowd was hearing the eternal Son of God.
ὁ ὄχλος ἤκουε τὸν αἰώνιον υἱὸν τοῦ θεοῦ.

We were going into the temple.
ἐβαίνομεν εἰς τὸ ἱερόν.

They were destroying the demons.
ἔλυον τὰ δαιμονια.

The apostles were destroying the evil demons.
οἱ ἀπόστολοι ἔλυον τὰ δαιμονια.

Lesson 24.1

	translation	part of speech	nouns only:	
			declension	gender
τό βιβλίον	the book	N	2nd	N
τό δαιμόνιον	the demon	N	2nd	N
τό ἔργον	the work	N	2nd	N
τό πλοῖον	the boat	N	2nd	N
ὁ ἁμαρτωλός	the sinner	N	2nd	M

Lesson 24.2

ὑπακούω	I obey	ὑπακούομεν	we obey
ὑπακούεις	you obey	ὑπακούετε	you obey
ὑπακούει	he obeys	ὑπακούουσι	they obey

ὑπήκουον	I was obeying	ὑπηκούομεν	we were obeying
ὑπήκουες	you were obeying	ὑπηκούετε	you were obeying
ὑπήκουε	he was obeying	ὑπήκουον	they were obeying

Lesson 24.3

ἄνθρωπος	ἄνθρωποι
ἀνθρώπου	ἀνθρώπων
ἀνθρώπῳ	ἀνθρώποις
ἄνθρωπον	ἀνθρώπους

δῶρον	δῶρα
δώρου	δώρων
δώρῳ	δώροις
δῶρον	δῶρα

ἀλήθεια	ἀλήθειαι
ἀληθείας	ἀληθειῶν
ἀληθείᾳ	ἀληθείαις
ἀλήθειαν	ἀληθείας

art   S   V   PN
οἱ ἀπόστολοι ἦσαν διδάσκαλοι.
The apostles were teachers.

art   S   V   PN/adj
ἡ εὐλογία ἦν καλή.
The blessing was good.

V (S)   PN
ἦμεν γεωργοί.
We were farmers.

V (S)   adj   PN
ἦτε δίκαιοι τυφλοί.
You were righteous blind men.

art   S   V   PN/adj
ἡ κώμη ἦν μικρά.
The village was small.

Lesson 24.4

	singular		plural	
Nom.	ἐγώ	I	ἡμεῖς	we
Gen.	μου	of me (mine)	ἡμῶν	of us (our)
Dat.	μοι	to me	ἡμῖν	to us
Acc.	με	me	ἡμᾶς	us

	singular		plural	
Nom.	σύ	you	ὑμεῖς	you
Gen.	σοῦ	of you (your)	ὑμῶν	of you (your)
Dat.	σοί	to you	ὑμῖν	to you
Acc.	σέ	you	ὑμᾶς	you

	Singular		
Nom.	ὁ	ἡ	τό
Gen.	τοῦ	τῆς	τοῦ
Dat.	τῷ	τῇ	τῷ
Acc.	τόν	τήν	τό
	Plural		
Nom.	οἱ	αἱ	τά
Gen.	τῶν	τῶν	τῶν
Dat.	τοῖς	ταῖς	τοῖς
Acc.	τούς	τάς	τά

ἤμην	I was	ἤμεν	we were
ἦς	you were	ἦτε	you were
ἦν	he, she, or it was	ἦσαν	they were

art   S   V   PN
The man was a farmer.
ὁ ἄνθρωπος ἦν γεωργός.

art   S   V   PN/adj
The children were faithful.
τὰ τέκνα ἦσαν πιστά.

S   V   adj   PN
We were good servants.
ἦμεν ἀγαθοὶ (καλοὶ) δοῦλοι.

art   S   V   PN/adj
The kingdom was wicked.
ἡ βασιλεία ἐν πονηρά.

S   V   PN
I was a teacher.
ἤμην διδάσκαλος.

Lesson 24.5

εἰμί	I am	ἐσμέν	we are
εἶ	you (s) are	ἐστέ	you are
ἐστί	he is	εἰσί	they are

ἤμην	I was	ἤμεν	we were
ἦς	you were	ἦτε	you were
ἦν	he, she, or it was	ἦσαν	they were

Lesson 25.1

θεραπεύω	I heal
εὑρίσκω	I find
κόπτω	I cut
ἀποθνήσκω	I die
ἡ Γαλιλαία	Galilee
κράζω	I cry out
ᾄδω	I sing
πίνω	I drink
ἡ παρουσία	the presence / the coming
ὁ γεωργός	the farmer
διώκω	I persecute
ὁ θρόνος	the throne
ἀντί (w/ gen)	instead of
ἀποκτείνω	I kill
δοξάζω	I glorify
χαίρω	I rejoice / am glad
ὀφείλω	I owe
ὑπακούω	I obey
ἡ εὐλογία	the praise / the blessing
γνωρίζω	I reveal

Lesson 25.2

γνωρίζω	I reveal	γνωρίζομεν	we reveal
γνωρίζεις	you reveal	γνωρίζετε	you reveal
γνωρίζει	he reveals	γνωρίζουσι	they reveal

ἐγνώριζον	I was revealing	ἐγνωρίζομεν	we were revealing
ἐγνώριζες	you were revealing	ἐγνωρίζετε	you were revealing
ἐγνώριζε	he was revealing	ἐγνώριζον	they were revealing

θεραπεύομεν	we heal
ἐγνώριζες	you were revealing
ἐδιώκετε	you were persecuting
καλύπτουσι	they hide

ὑπήκουον	I was obeying / they were obeying
εὑρίσκεις	you find
ἀποστέλλει	he sends
ἔκοπτε	he was cutting
ἀπήθνησκον	I was dying / they were dying
ἀποκτείνομεν	we kill

Lesson 25.3

ἄνθρωπος	Nominative	ἄνθρωποι
ἀνθρώπου	Genitive	ἀνθρώπων
ἀνθρώπῳ	Dative	ἀνθρώποις
ἄνθρωπον	Accusative	ἀνθρώπους

δῶρον	δῶρα
δώρου	δώρων
δώρῳ	δώροις
δῶρον	δῶρα

ἀλήθεια	ἀλήθειαι
ἀληθείας	ἀληθειῶν
ἀληθείᾳ	ἀληθείαις
ἀλήθειαν	ἀληθείας

We cut	κόπτομεν
You (p) were glorifying	ἐδοξάζετε
We were hiding	ἐκαλύπτομεν
They sing	ᾄδουσι
He was crying out	ἔκραζε
You (s) owe	ὀφείλεις
I was rejoicing	ἔχαιρον
They were killing	ἀπέκτεινον
We find	εὑρίσκομεν
You (p) persecute	διώκετε

Lesson 25.4

	singular		plural	
Nom.	εγώ	I	ἡμεῖς	we
Gen.	μου	of me (mine)	ἡμῶν	of us (our)
Dat.	μοι	to me	ἡμῖν	to us
Acc.	με	me	ἡμᾶς	us

	singular		plural	
Nom.	σύ	you	ὑμεῖς	you
Gen.	σοῦ	of you (your)	ὑμῶν	of you (your)
Dat.	σοί	to you	ὑμῖν	to you
Acc.	σέ	you	ὑμᾶς	you

	Singular		
Nom.	ὁ	ἡ	τό
Gen.	τοῦ	τῆς	τοῦ
Dat.	τῷ	τῇ	τῷ
Acc.	τόν	τήν	τό
	Plural		
Nom.	οἱ	αἱ	τά
Gen.	τῶν	τῶν	τῶν
Dat.	τοῖς	ταῖς	τοῖς
Acc.	τούς	τάς	τά

	Singular		
Nom.	πρῶτος	πρώτη	πρῶτον
Gen.	πρώτου	πρώτης	πρώτου
Dat.	πρώτῳ	πρώτῃ	πρώτῳ
Acc.	πρῶτον	πρώτην	πρῶτον
	Plural		
Nom.	πρῶτοι	πρῶται	πρῶτα
Gen.	πρώτων	πρώτων	πρώτων
Dat.	πρώτοις	πρώταις	πρώτοις
Acc.	πρώτους	πρώτας	πρῶτα

art adj   S   V   art   DO
ὁ κακὸς ἄνθρωπος ἐδίωκε τὸν ἀπόστολον.
The bad man was persecuting the apostle.

   V (S)   con   V (S)   DO
ἐχαίρομεν καὶ ᾔδομεν εὐλογίας.
We were rejoicing and singing blessings.

art   S   V   art   DO   prep art
ὁ γεωργὸς εὑρίσκει τὰ πρόβατα ἐν τῷ
        OP
ἀγρῷ.
The farmer finds the sheep in the field.

art   S   V   art   DO   art
οἱ ἄνθρωποι ὑπήκουον τοὺς λογοὺς τοῦ
    poss
θεοῦ.
The men were obeying the words of God.

art   S   V   art   DO
ὁ κύριος γνωρίζει τὴν ἀλήθειαν.
The Lord reaveals the truth.

Lesson 25.5

Textbook:
What is this parable about?
A farmer and his sheep
What has the farmer lost?
He has lost his sheep.
Where does the farmer call for the sheep?
He calls in the fields and in the villages.
What does the farmer do when he finds the sheep?
He rejoices.

Workbook:

ε	γ	ν	ω	ρ	ι	ζ	ο	ν		υ			
β		ε		η	μ	η	ν		π				
α		θ	ε	σ		ε		η					
λ		ε	θ	α		β		κ					
λ		λ	ε	ν	ε	χ	α	ι	ρ	ο	μ	ε	ν
ε		ο	λ	λ		ι		υ					
		ν	ο	υ		ν		ε					
		μ		ε		ε		ι					
		ε		ς		τ		ς					
		ν				ε							

ἐγνώριζον	they were revealing
ἤμην	I was
ἦσαν	they were
ἔβαλλε	he was throwing
ἔθελον	I was wishing
ἐχαίρομεν	we were rejoicing
ὑπήκουες	you (s) were obeying
ἐβαίνετε	you (p) were going
ἔλυες	you (s) were loosing
ἐθέλομεν	we were wishing

Lesson 26.1

	translation	part of speech	nouns only: declension	gender
τό τέκνον	the child	N	2nd	N
τό εὐαγγέλιον	the gospel	N	2nd	N
τό πρόσωπον	the face	N	2nd	N
τό ἱερόν	the temple	N	2nd	N
τό δῶρον	the gift	N	2nd	N

Lesson 26.2

καλύπτω	I hide	καλύπτομεν	we hide
καλύπτεις	you hide	καλύπτετε	you hide
καλύπτει	he hides	καλύπτουσι	they hide

ἐκάλυπτον	I was hiding	ἐκαλύπτομεν	we were hiding
ἐκάλυπτες	you were hiding	ἐκαλύπτετε	you were hiding
ἐκάλυπτε	he was hiding	ἐκαλυπτον	they were hiding

ἀποκρίνομαι	I answer	ἀποκρινόμεθα	we answer
ἀποκρίνῃ	you answer	ἀποκρίνεσθε	you answer
ἀποκρίνεται	he answers	ἀποκρίνονται	they answer

ἄρχομαι	I begin	ἀρχόμεθα	we begin
ἄρχῃ	you begin	ἄρχεσθε	you begin
ἄρχεται	he begins	ἄρχονται	they begin

Lesson 26.3

ἀποκρίνονται	they answer
γίνῃ	you become
ἔρχεσθε	you come/you go
δεχόμεθα	we receive
ἄρχεται	he begins

Lesson 26.4

Singular			
Nom.	ὁ	ἡ	τό
Gen.	τοῦ	τῆς	τοῦ
Dat.	τῷ	τῇ	τῷ
Acc.	τόν	τήν	τό
Plural			
Nom.	οἱ	αἱ	τά
Gen.	τῶν	τῶν	τῶν
Dat.	τοῖς	ταῖς	τοῖς
Acc.	τούς	τάς	τά

	Singular		
Nom.	ἀγαθός	ἀγαθή	ἀγαθόν
Gen.	ἀγαθοῦ	ἀγαθῆς	ἀγαθοῦ
Dat.	ἀγαθῷ	ἀγαθῇ	ἀγαθῷ
Acc.	ἀγαθόν	ἀγαθήν	ἀγαθόν
	Plural		
Nom.	ἀγαθοί	ἀγαθαί	ἀγαθά
Gen.	ἀγαθῶν	ἀγαθῶν	ἀγαθῶν
Dat.	ἀγαθοῖς	ἀγαθαῖς	ἀγαθοῖς
Acc.	ἀγαθούς	ἀγαθάς	ἀγαθά

We go	ἐρχόμεθα
You (s) receive	δέχῃ
He answers	ἀποκρίνεται
They become	δέχονται
You(p) begin	ἄρχεσθε

Lesson 27.1

	translation	part of speech	nouns only: declension	gender
πέμπω	I send	V		
φέρω	I bring	V		
βαπτίζω	I baptize	V		
κρίνω	I judge	V		
ὁ διδάσκαλος	the teacher	N	2nd	M

Lesson 27.2

λύω	I loose	λύομεν	we loose
λύεις	you loose	λύετε	you loose
λύει	he looses	λύουσι	they loose

ἔλυον	I was loosing	ἐλύομεν	we were loosing
ἔλυες	you were loosing	ἐλύετε	you were loosing
ἔλυε	he was loosing	ἔλυον	they were loosing

λογίζομαι	I think	λογιζόμεθα	we think
λογίζῃ	you think	λογίζεσθε	you think
λογίζεται	he thinks	λογίζονται	they think

εὐαγγελιζόμεθα	we preach
πιστεύομεν	we believe
βούλεσθε	you wish, desire
ἔλυον	I was loosing (destroying)/ they were loosing

βαίνεις	you go
ἐργάζῃ	you work
ἐβάλλετε	you were throwing
λογίζεται	he thinks
χαρίζονται	they forgive
ἀκούουσι	they hear

Lesson 27.3

ἄνθρωπος	ἄνθρωποι
ἀνθρώπου	ἀνθρώπων
ἀνθρώπῳ	ἀνθρώποις
ἄνθρωπον	ἀνθρώπους

δῶρον	δῶρα
δώρου	δώρων
δώρῳ	δώροις
δῶρον	δῶρα

ἀλήθεια	ἀλήθειαι
ἀληθείας	ἀληθειῶν
ἀληθείᾳ	ἀληθείαις
ἀλήθειαν	ἀληθείας

βούλομαι	I wish	βουλόμεθα	we wish
βούλῃ	you wish	βούλεσθε	you wish
βούλεται	he wishes	βούλονται	they wish

λογίζομαι	I think	λογιζόμεθα	we think
λογίζῃ	you think	λογίζεσθε	you think
λογίζεται	he thinks	λογίζονται	they think

V (S)   art DO art IO
εὐαγγελιζόμεθα τὸν λόγον τῷ ὄχλῳ.
We preach the word to the crowd.

art S V   art DO
ὁ θεὸς χαρίζεται τοὺς ἁμαρτωλούς.
God forgives the sinners.

V (S) con art S V PN/adj
λογίζεσθε ὅτι οἱ ἄνθρωποί εἰσι πιστοί.
You think that men are faithful.

V (S) art adj DO prep OP
δέχομαι τὰ καλὰ δῶρα ἀπὸ θεοῦ.
I receive the good gifts from God.

art S   V   art   DO
ὁ γεωργὸς ἀποκρίνεται τῷ τέκνῳ.
The farmer answers the child.

Lesson 27.4

	singular		plural	
Nom.	εγώ	I	ἡμεῖς	we
Gen.	μου	of me (mine)	ἡμῶν	of us (our)
Dat.	μοι	to me	ἡμῖν	to us
Acc.	με	me	ἡμᾶς	us

	singular		plural	
Nom.	σύ	you	ὑμεῖς	you
Gen.	σοῦ	of you (your)	ὑμῶν	of you (your)
Dat.	σοί	to you	ὑμῖν	to you
Acc.	σέ	you	ὑμᾶς	you

	Singular		
Nom.	ὁ	ἡ	τό
Gen.	τοῦ	τῆς	τοῦ
Dat.	τῷ	τῇ	τῷ
Acc.	τόν	τήν	τό
	Plural		
Nom.	οἱ	αἱ	τά
Gen.	τῶν	τῶν	τῶν
Dat.	τοῖς	ταῖς	τοῖς
Acc.	τούς	τάς	τά

χαρίζομαι	I forgive	χαριζόμεθα	we forgive
χαρίζῃ	you forgive	χαρίζεσθε	you forgive
χαρίζεται	he forgives	χαρίζονται	they forgive

γνωρίζω	I reveal	γνωρίζομεν	we reveal
γνωρίζεις	you reveal	γνωρίζετε	you reveal
γνωρίζει	he reveals	γνωρίζουσι	they reveal

art   S   V   art   DO   art IO
The men preach the gospel to the slaves.
οἱ ἄνθρωποι εὐαγγελίζονται τὸ εὐαγγέλιον
τοῖς δουλοῖς.

S   V   prep art   OP
Farmers work in the fields.
οἱ γεωργοὶ ἐργάζονται ἐν τοῖς ἀγροῖς.

S   V prep   art   OP
We go out of the house.
ἐρχόμεθα ἐκ τοῦ οἴκου (τῆς οικίας).

art   S   V   art   DO
The apostle answers the blind man.
ὁ ἀπόστολος ἀποκίρνεται τῷ τυφλῷ.

art   S   V   art   DO
The lord forgives the slaves.
ὁ κύριος χαρίζεται τοὺς δούλους.

Lesson 28.1

	translation	part of speech	nouns only: declension	gender
ὁ οὐρανός	the heaven	N	2ⁿᵈ	M
ὁ τόπος	the place	N	2ⁿᵈ	M
ἐγείρω	I raise up	V		
ἄγω	I lead	V		
μένω	I remain	V		

Lesson 28.2

βλέπω	I see	βλέπομεν	we see
βλέπεις	you see	βλέπετε	you see
βλέπει	he sees	βλέπουσι	they see

ἔβλεπον	I was seeing	ἐβλέπομεν	we were seeing
ἔβλεπες	you were seeing	ἐβλέπετε	you were seeing
ἔβλεπε	he was seeing	ἔβλεπον	they were seeing

ἔρχομαι	I come/ go	ἐρχόμεθα	we come/ go
ἔρχῃ	you come/ go	ἔρχεσθε	you come/ go
ἔρχεται	he comes/ goes	ἔρχονται	they come/ go

We go out	ἐξερχόμεθα
They go in	εἰσέρχονται
You (s) come	ἔρχῃ
You (p) go	ἔρχεσθε
He goes through	διέρχεται

Lesson 28.3

V (S)   art   DO   con   V (S)   art
διερχόμεθα τὸν τόπον καὶ εἰσερχόμεθα
τὴν
   DO
κώμην.
We go through the place and we go into the
village.

art   S   V   prep   art   OP
οἱ γεωργοὶ λογίζονται περὶ τοῦ ἔργου.
The farmers think about the work.

V (S)   art   DO   con   V (S)   PN/adj
ἦγον τὰ τέκνα ὅτι ἦσαν μικρά.
I was (or they were) leading the children because
they were little.

V   con+S/pro   V
εἰσέρχομαι κἀγὼ ἐξέρχομαι.
I go in and I go out.

art   S   V   DO
οἱ ἀπόστολοι ἤγειρον τοὺς ἀνθρώπους.
The apostles were raising up the men.

Lesson 28.4

	singular		plural	
Nom.	εγώ	I	ἡμεῖς	we
Gen.	μου	of me (mine)	ἡμῶν	of us (our)
Dat.	μοι	to me	ἡμῖν	to us
Acc.	με	me	ἡμᾶς	us

	singular		plural	
Nom.	σύ	you	ὑμεῖς	you
Gen.	σοῦ	of you (your)	ὑμῶν	of you (your)
Dat.	σοί	to you	ὑμῖν	to you
Acc.	σέ	you	ὑμᾶς	you

	Singular		
Nom.	ὁ	ἡ	τό
Gen.	τοῦ	τῆς	τοῦ
Dat.	τῷ	τῇ	τῷ
Acc.	τόν	τήν	τό

	Plural		
Nom.	οἱ	αἱ	τά
Gen.	τῶν	τῶν	τῶν
Dat.	τοῖς	ταῖς	τοῖς
Acc.	τούς	τάς	τά

	Singular		
Nom.	καλός	καλή	καλόν
Gen.	καλοῦ	καλῆς	καλοῦ
Dat.	καλῷ	καλῇ	καλῷ
Acc.	καλόν	καλήν	καλόν
	Plural		
Nom.	καλοί	καλαί	καλά
Gen.	καλῶν	καλῶν	καλῶν
Dat.	καλοῖς	καλαῖς	καλοῖς
Acc.	καλούς	καλάς	καλά

S   _V_   art   DO   con   S   _V_   art   DO
We go through the field and we go into the house.
διερχόμεθα τὸν ἀγρὸν καὶ εἰσερχόμεθα τὸν
οἶκον (τὴν οἰκίαν)

art   adj   S   _V_   DO
The faithful men were glorifying God.
οἱ πιστοὶ ἄνθρωποι ἐδόξαζον τὸν θεόν.

art   S   _V_   art   DO
The children go out of the church.
τὰ τέκνα εἰσέρχονται τὴν ἐκκλησίαν.

art   S   V   con   S   V   PN/adj
The crowd hears that God is faithful.
ὁ ὄχλος ἀκούει ὅτι θεός ἐστι πιστός.

S   V   art   DO
You (p) enter the kingdom.
εἰσέρχεσθε τὴν βασιλείαν.

Lesson 29.1

The first three vocabulary words for today are __nouns__.
They belong to the __first__ declension and are __masculine.__
The last two vocabulary words for today are __adverbs__.

	translation	part of speech	nouns only:	
			declension	gender
ὁ θάνατος	the death	N	2nd	M
ὁ οἶκος	the house	N	2nd	M
ὁ υἱός	the son	N	2nd	M
ὁ κύριος	the lord	N	2nd	M
ὁ λίθος	the stone	N	2nd	M

Lesson 29.2

ἄγω	ἄγομεν	δέχομαι	δεχόμεθα
ἄγεις	ἄγετε	δέχῃ	δέχεσθε
ἄγει	ἄγουσι	δεχεται	δέχονται

ἤμην	I was	ἦμεν	we were
ἦς	you were	ἦτε	you were
ἦν	he, she, or it was	ἦσαν	they were

μαθητής	Nominative	μαθηταί
μαθητοῦ	Genitive	μαθητῶν
μαθητῇ	Dative	μαθηταῖς
μαθητήν	Accusative	μαθητάς

Lesson 29.3

ἄνθρωπος	ἄνθρωποι
ἀνθρώπου	ἀνθρώπων
ἀνθρώπῳ	ἀνθρώποις
ἄνθρωπον	ἀνθρώπους

δῶρον	δῶρα
δώρου	δώρων
δώρῳ	δώροις
δῶρον	δῶρα

ἀλήθεια	ἀλήθειαι
ἀληθείας	ἀληθειῶν
ἀληθείᾳ	ἀληθείαις
ἀλήθειαν	ἀληθείας

the holy prophet (accusative case)
τὸν ἅγιον προφήτην

a bad young man (nominative case)
κακὸς νεανίας

of the other disciple
τοῦ ἄλλου μαθητοῦ

to/for the last young man
τῷ ἐσχάτῳ νεανίᾳ

Lesson 29.4

	singular		plural	
Nom.	εγώ	I	ἡμεῖς	we
Gen.	μου	of me (mine)	ἡμῶν	of us (our)
Dat.	μοι	to me	ἡμῖν	to us
Acc.	με	me	ἡμᾶς	us

	singular		plural	
Nom.	σύ	you	ὑμεῖς	you
Gen.	σοῦ	of you (your)	ὑμῶν	of you (your)
Dat.	σοί	to you	ὑμῖν	to you
Acc.	σέ	you	ὑμᾶς	you

	Singular		
Nom.	ὁ	ἡ	τό
Gen.	τοῦ	τῆς	τοῦ
Dat.	τῷ	τῇ	τῷ
Acc.	τόν	τήν	τό
	Plural		
Nom.	οἱ	αἱ	τά
Gen.	τῶν	τῶν	τῶν
Dat.	τοῖς	ταῖς	τοῖς
Acc.	τούς	τάς	τά

ὁ νεανίας ἦν οὔπω μαθητής.
The young man was not yet a disciple.

ἀκούομεν περὶ τοῦ θανάτου τοῦ πιστοῦ προφήτου.
We hear about the death of the faithful prophet.

οὔπω εἰσέρχομαι τὸν οἶκον σὺν τῷ νεανίᾳ.
I do not yet enter the house with the young man.

νῦν ὁ λίθος ἐστιν ἐν τῷ ἀγρῷ.
Now the stone is in the field.

ὁ μαθητής εὐαγγελίζεται τὴν ἀλήθειαν τοῖς υἱοῖς.
The disciple preaches the truth to the sons.

Lesson 30.1

ἀποκρίνομαι	I answer
ἄρχομαι	I begin
λογίζομαι	I think
εὐαγγελίζομαι	I preach
βούλομαι	I wish
εἰσέρχομαι	I go in / enter
διέρχομαι	I go through
ὁ μαθητής	the disciple
ὁ νεανίας	the young man
οὔπω	not yet
γίνομαι	I become
δέχομαι	I receive
ἐργάζομαι	I work
χαρίζομαι	I forgive
ἔρχομαι	I come / I go
ἐξέρχομαι	I go out
κἀγώ	and I
ὁ προφήτης	the prophet
νῦν	now

Lesson 30.2

διώκω	I persecute	διώκομεν	we persecute
διώκεις	you persecute	διώκετε	you persecute
διώκει	he persecutes	διώκουσι	they persecute

γίνομαι	I become	γινόμεθα	we become
γίνῃ	you become	γίνεσθε	you become
γίνεται	he becomes	γίνονται	they become

ἤμην	I was	ἦμεν	we were
ἦς	you were	ἦτε	you were
ἦν	he, she, or it was	ἦσαν	they were

Lesson 30.3

ἄνθρωπος	ἄνθρωποι
ἀνθρώπου	ἀνθρώπων
ἀνθρώπῳ	ἀνθρώποις
ἄνθρωπον	ἀνθρώπους

δῶρον	δῶρα
δώρου	δώρων
δώρῳ	δώροις
δῶρον	δῶρα

ἀλήθεια	ἀλήθειαι
ἀληθείας	ἀληθειῶν
ἀληθείᾳ	ἀληθείαις
ἀλήθειαν	ἀληθείας

μαθητής	μαθηταί
μαθητοῦ	μαθητῶν
μαθητῇ	μαθηταῖς
μαθητήν	μαθητάς

προφήτης	προφῆται
προφήτου	προφητῶν
προφήτῃ	προφήταις
προφήτην	προφήτας

νεανίας	νεανίαι
νεανίου	νεανιῶν
νεανίᾳ	νεανίαις
νεανίαν	νεανίας

Lesson 30.4

	singular		plural	
Nom.	εγώ	I	ἡμεῖς	we
Gen.	μου	of me (mine)	ἡμῶν	of us (our)
Dat.	μοι	to me	ἡμῖν	to us
Acc.	με	me	ἡμᾶς	us

	singular		plural	
Nom.	σύ	you	ὑμεῖς	you
Gen.	σοῦ	of you (your)	ὑμῶν	of you (your)
Dat.	σοί	to you	ὑμῖν	to you
Acc.	σέ	you	ὑμᾶς	you

	Singular		
Nom.	ὁ	ἡ	τό
Gen.	τοῦ	τῆς	τοῦ
Dat.	τῷ	τῇ	τῷ
Acc.	τόν	τήν	τό
	Plural		
Nom.	οἱ	αἱ	τά
Gen.	τῶν	τῶν	τῶν
Dat.	τοῖς	ταῖς	τοῖς
Acc.	τούς	τάς	τά

ὁ πρῶτος μαθητὴς ἀποκρίνεται τῷ
δευτέρῳ μαθητῇ.
The first disciple answers the second disciple.

οἱ νεανίαι οὔπω ἐργάζονται ἐν τοῖς
ἀγροῖς.
The young men no longer work in the fields.

ὁ γεωργός   χαρίζεται τοὺς νεανίας.
The farmer forgives the young men.

ὁ προφήτης ἐξέρχεται κἀγὼ εἰσέρχομαι.
The prophet goes out and goes in.

γινόμεθα ἄνθρωποι τοῦ θεοῦ.
We become men of God.

Lesson 30.5

Textbook:
Whom does the disciple baptize?
> *The disciple baptizes the son of the lord of the
> kingdom.*
What does the father (the lord) do?
> *The father rejoices with his son.*
What does the young man become?
> *He becomes a disciple of Christ.*
What does he think about?
> *He thinks about God.*